Revolu
Optimism,
Western Nihilism

Andre Vltchek

Badak Merah Semesta

2018

Andre Vltchek

Revolutionary Optimism,
Western Nihilism,

Cover Photos by: Andre Vltchek
Cover Design by: Rossie Indira
Layout by: Rossie Indira

First edition, 2018

Published by PT. Badak Merah Semesta
Jl. Madrasah Azziyadah 16, Jakarta
http://badak-merah.weebly.com
email: badak.merah.press@gmail.com

ISBN: 978-602-50954-1-2

Revolutionary Optimism, Western Nihilism

Andre Vltchek

By the same author

Exposing Lies of the Empire
Fighting Against Western Imperialism
On Western Terrorism: From Hiroshima to
Drone Warfare (with Noam Chomsky)
The World Order and Revolution! (with
Christopher Black & Peter Koenig)
Western Terror: From Potosi to Baghdad
Indonesia: Archipelago of Fear
Exile (with Pramoedya Ananta Toer &
Rossie Indira)
Oceania – Neocolonialism, Nukes & Bones

Fiction:
Aurora
Point of No Return
Nalezeny
Plays: 'Ghosts of Valparaiso' and
'Conversations with James'

Andre Vltchek

Content

1

Revolutionary Optimism and Western Nihilism

How dreadfully depressing life has become in almost all of the Western cities! How awful and sad.

It is not that these cities are not rich; they are. Of course things are deteriorating there, the infrastructure is crumbling and there are signs of social inequality, even misery, at every corner. But if compared to almost all other parts of the world, the wealth of the Western cities still appears to be shocking, almost grotesque.

The affluence does not guarantee contentment, happiness or optimism.

Spend an entire day strolling through London or Paris, and pay close attention to people. You will repeatedly stumble over passive aggressive behavior, over frustration and desperate downcast glances, over omnipresent sadness.

In all those once great [imperialist] cities, what is missing is life. Euphoria, warmth, poetry and yes – love – are all in extremely short supply there.

Wherever you walk, all around, the buildings are monumental, and boutiques are overflowing with elegant merchandize. At night, bright lights shine brilliantly. Yet the faces of people are gray. Even when forming couples, even when in groups, human beings appear to be thoroughly atomized, like the sculptures of Giacometti.

Talk to people, and you'll most likely encounter confusion, depression, and uncertainty. 'Refined' sarcasm, and sometimes a bogus urban politeness are like thin bandages that are trying to conceal the most horrifying anxieties and thoroughly unbearable loneliness of those 'lost' human souls.

Purposelessness is intertwined with passivity. In the West, it is increasingly hard to find someone that is truly committed: politically, intellectually or even emotionally. Big feelings are now seen as frightening; both men and women reject them. Grand gestures are increasingly looked down upon, or even ridiculed. Dreams are becoming tiny, shy and always 'down to earth', and even those are lately extremely well concealed. Even to daydream is seen as something 'irrational' and outdated.

To a stranger who comes from afar, it appears to be a sad, unnatural, brutally restrained and to a great extent, a pitiful world.

Tens of millions of adult men and women, some well educated, 'do not know what to do with their lives'. They take courses or go 'back to school' in order to fill the void, and to 'discover what they want to do' with their existence. It is all self-serving, as there appear to be no greater aspirations anywhere. Most of the efforts begin and end with each particular individual.

Nobody sacrifices himself or herself for others, for society, for humanity, for the cause, or even for the 'other half', anymore.

In fact, even the concept of the 'other half' is disappearing. Relationships are increasingly 'distant', each person searching for his or her 'space', demanding independence even in those rare moments of togetherness. There are no 'two halves of one'; instead there are 'two fully independent individuals', co-existing in a relative proximity, sometimes physically touching, sometimes not, but mostly entirely on their own.

In the Western capitals, the egocentricity, even total obsession with one's personal needs, is brought to a surreal extreme.

Psychologically, it can only be described as a twisted, unnatural and truly pathological world.

Surrounded by this bizarre pseudo reality, many formerly healthy individuals eventually feel, or even become, mentally ill. Then, paradoxically, they get convinced that they have no choice, and they embark on seeking 'professional help', so they can re-join the ranks of the 'normal', read 'thoroughly subdued' citizens. In most cases, instead of continuously rebelling, instead of waging personal wars against the state of things, the individuals who are still at least to some extent different, get so frightened by being in the minority that they give up, surrender voluntarily, and identify themselves as 'abnormal'. There is always plenty of 'help' available for those who 'repent' and 'choose' to join the ranks of obedient masses.

Short sparks of freedom experienced by those who are still capable of at least some imagination, of dreaming about a true and natural world, get rapidly extinguished.

Then, in a short instant, everything gets irreversibly lost. It may appear as some horror film, but it is not, it is the true reality of life in the West.

***

I cannot function in such an environment for more than a few days. If forced, I could last in London or Paris for two weeks at most, but only while operating on some 'emergency mode', unable to write, to create and to function 'normally'. I cannot imagine 'being in love' in a place like that. I cannot imagine reading a book of poetry. I cannot imagine writing a revolutionary essay there. I cannot imagine laughing, loudly, happily, freely.

While briefly working in London, Paris or New York, the coldness, purposelessness, and chronic lack of passion and of all basic human emotions, is having a tremendously exhausting effect on me, derailing my creativity and drowning me in useless, pathetic existentialist dilemmas.

After one week there, I'm simply beginning to get influenced by that awful environment: I'm starting to think about myself excessively, 'listening to *my feelings*', instead of considering the feelings of the others. My duties towards humanity get neglected. I put on hold everything that I otherwise consider essential. My revolutionary edge loses its sharpness. My optimism begins to evaporate. My determination to struggle for a better world begins to weaken.

This is when I know: it is time to run, to run away. Fast, very fast! It is time to pull myself from the stale emotional swamp, to slam the door behind the intellectual bordello, and to escape from the terrifying meaninglessness that is marked with injured, even wasted lives.

I cannot fight for those people from within, only from outside. Our way of thinking and feeling do not match. When they get out and visit 'my universe', they bring with them resilient prejudices: they do not register what they see and hear, they stick to what they were indoctrinated with, for years and decades. I cannot convince them of anything, simply because they are refusing to see.

***

For me personally there are not many significant things that I can do in Western cities. Periodically I come to sign one or two book contracts, to screen my films, or to speak briefly at some university, but I don't see any point of doing much more. In the West, it is hard to find any meaningful struggle. Most struggles there are not internationalist; instead they are selfish, West-oriented in nature. Almost no true courage, no profound kindness, no passion, and no rebellion remain. On closer examination, there is actually no life there; no life as we human beings used to perceive it, and as we still understand it in many other parts of the world.

Nihilism rules. Was this mental state, this collective condition or illness something that has been inflicted on purpose by the regime? I don't know. I cannot yet answer this question. But it is essential to ask, and to try to understand.

Whatever it is, it is extremely effective – negatively effective but effective nevertheless.

Carl Gustav Jung, a renowned Swiss psychologist and psychiatrist, diagnosed Western culture as 'pathological', right after WWII. But instead of trying to comprehend its own abysmal condition, instead of trying to get better, even well, Western culture is actually made to expand, to rapidly spread to many other parts of the world, dangerously contaminating healthy societies and nations.

It has to be stopped. I say it because I do love this life, the life, which still exists outside the Western realm; I'm intoxicated with it, obsessed with it. I live it to the fullest, with great delight, enjoying every moment of it.

I know the world, from the 'Southern Cone' of South America, to Oceania, the Middle East, to the most god-forsaken corners of Africa and Asia. It is a truly tremendous world, full of beauty and diversity, and hope.

The more I see and know, the more I realize that I absolutely cannot exist without a struggle, without a good fight, without great passions and love, and without purpose; basically without all that the West is trying to reduce to nothing, to make irrelevant, obsolete and ridiculous.

My entire being is rebelling against the awful nihilism and dark pessimism that is being injected almost everywhere by Western culture. I'm violently allergic to it. I refuse to accept it. I refuse to succumb to it.

I see people, good people, talented people, wonderful people, getting contaminated, having their lives ruined. I see them abandoning great battles, abandoning their great loves. I see them choosing selfishness and their 'space' and 'personal feelings' over deep affection and inseparability, opting for meaningless careers over great adventures of epic battles for humanity and better world.

Lives are being ruined one by one, and by millions, every moment and every day. Lives that could have been full of beauty, full of joy, of love, full of searching, of creativity and uniqueness, of meaning and purpose, but instead are reduced to thorough meaninglessness. People living such lives are performing tasks and jobs by inertia, respecting without questioning all behavior patterns ordered by the regime, and obeying countless grotesque laws and regulations.

They cannot walk on their own feet, anymore. They have been made fully submissive. Their lives are over.

That is because the courage of the people in the West has been broken. It is because they have been reduced to a crowd of obedient subjects, submissive to the destructive and morally defunct Empire.

They have lost the ability to think for themselves. They have lost courage to feel.

As a result, because the West has such an enormous influence on the rest of the world, the entire humanity is in grave danger, is suffering, and is losing its natural bearing.

In such a society, a person overflowing with passion, a person fully committed and true to his or her cause can never be taken seriously. It is because in a society like this, only deep nihilism and cynicism are accepted and respected.

In such a society, a revolution or a rebellion could hardly go beyond the pub or a living room couch.

A person, who is still capable of loving in such an emotionally constipating and twisted environment, is usually seen as a buffoon, even as a 'suspicious and sinister element'. It is common for him or for her to be ridiculed and rejected.

Obedient and cowardly masses hate those who are different. They distrust people who stand tall and who are still capable of fighting, people who know perfectly well what their goals are, people who *do* and not just talk, and those who find it easy to throw their entire life, without the slightest hesitation, at the feet of a beloved person or an honorable cause.

Such individuals terrify and irritate those suave, submissive and shallow crowds in Western capitals. As a punishment, they get deserted and divorced, ostracized, socially exiled and demonized. Some end up getting attacked, even thoroughly destroyed.

The result is: there is no culture, anywhere on Earth, so banal, so uniformed and so obedient as that which is now regulating the West. Lately, nothing of revolutionary intellectual significance is flowing from Europe and North America, as there are hardly any detectable unorthodox ways of thinking or perceptions of the world there.

The dialogues and debates are flowing only through fully anticipated and well-regulated channels, and needless to say they fluctuate only marginally and through the fully 'pre-approved' frequencies.

***

What is on the other side of the barricade?

I don't want to glorify our revolutionary countries and movements.

I don't even want to write that we are the "exact opposite" of that entire nightmare that has been created by the West. We are not. And we are far from being perfect.

But we are alive if not always well, we

are standing, trying to advance this wonderful 'project' called humanity, attempting to save our planet from Western imperialism, its nihilist gloom, as well as absolute environmental disaster.

We are considering many different ways forward. We have never rejected socialism and Communism, and we are studying various moderate and controlled forms of capitalism. The advantages and disadvantages of the so-called 'mixed economy' are being discussed and evaluated.

We fight, but because we are much less brutal, orthodox and dogmatic than the West, we often lose, as we recently (and hopefully only temporarily) lost in Brazil and Argentina. We also win, again and again. As this essay goes to print, we are celebrating in Ecuador and El Salvador.

Unlike in the West, in such places like China, Russia and Latin America, our debates about the political and economic future are vibrant, even stormy. Our art is engaged, helping to search for the best humanist concepts. Our thinkers are alert, compassionate and innovative, and our songs and poems are great, full of desire and fire, overflowing with love and longing.

Our countries do not steal from anyone; they don't overthrow governments in the opposite parts of the world, they do not undertake massive military invasions. What we have is ours; it is what we have created, produced and sown with our own hands. It is not always much, but we are proud of it, because no one had to die for it, and no one had to be enslaved.

Our hearts are purer. They are not always absolutely pure, but purer than those in the West are. We do not abandon those whom we love, even if they fall, get injured, or cannot walk any longer. Our women do not abandon their men, especially those who are in the middle of fighting for a better world. Our men do not abandon their women, even when they are in deep pain or despair. We know whom and what we love, and we know whom and what we hate: in this we rarely get 'confused'.

We are much simpler than those living in the West. In many ways, we are also much deeper.

We respect hard work, especially work that helps to improve the lives of millions, not just our own lives, or the lives of our families.

We try to keep our promises. We don't always succeed in keeping them, as we are only humans, but we are trying, and most of the times we are managing to.

Things are not always exactly like this, but often they are. And when "things are like this", it means that there is at least some hope and optimism and often even great joy.

Optimism is essential for any progress. No revolution could succeed without tremendous enthusiasm, as no love could. No revolution and no love could be built on depression, despair and defeatism.

Even in the middle of the ashes to which imperialism has reduced our world, a true revolutionary and a true poet can always at least find some hope. It will not be easy, not easy at all, but definitely not impossible. Nothing is ever lost in this life, for as long as our hearts are beating.

***

The state in which our world is right now is dreadful. It often feels that one more step in a wrong direction, another false turn, and everything will finally collapse, irreversibly. It is easy, extremely easy, to give up, to throw everything up into the air, and to land on a couch with a six-pack of beer, or to simply declare "there is nothing that can be done", and then resume one's meaningless life routine.

Western nihilism has already done its devastating work: it has landed tens of millions of thinking beings on their proverbial couches of spinelessness. It has spread pessimism and gloom, and a general belief that things can never improve, anymore. It has maneuvered people into refusing to 'accept labels', into rejecting progressive ideologies, and into a pathological distrust of any power. The "all politicians are the same" slogan could be translated clearly into: "We all know that our Western rulers are gangsters, but do not expect anything else from those in other parts of the world." "All people are the same" reads: "The West has been plundering and murdering hundreds of millions, but don't expect anything better from Asians, Latin Americans or Africans".

This irrational, cynical negativism

already domesticated in virtually all countries of the West, and has successfully been exported to many colonies, even to such places as Afghanistan, where people have been suffering incessantly from crimes committed by the West.

Its goal is evident: to prevent people from taking action and to convince them that any rebellion is futile. Such attitudes are brutally and successfully choking all hopes.

In the meantime, collateral damage is mounting. Metastases of the passivity and nihilistic cancers which are being spread by the Western regime are already attacking even that very human ability to love, to commit to a person or to a cause, and to stand by one's pledges and obligations.

In the West and in its colonies, courage has lost its entire luster. The Empire has managed to reverse the whole scale of human values, which was firmly and naturally in place on all the continents and in all cultures, for centuries and millennia. All of a sudden, submission and obedience have come to vogue.

It often feels that if the trend is not reversed soon, people will increasingly live like mice: constantly scared, neurotic, unreliable, depressed, passive, unable to identify true greatness, and unwilling to join those who are still pulling our world and humanity forward.

Billions of lives will get wasted. Billions of lives are already being wasted.

***

Some of us write about invasions, coups and dictatorships imposed by the Empire. However, almost nothing is being written about this tremendous and silent genocide that is breaking the human spirit and optimism, throwing entire nations into a dark depression and gloom. But it is taking place, even as these lines are being penned. It is happening everywhere, even in such places as London, Paris and New York, or more precisely, especially there.

In those glorified but unfortunate places, fear of great emotions has already been deeply rooted. Originality, courage and determination are now evoking fear. Great love, great gestures and unorthodox dreams are all observed with panic and mistrust.

But no progress, no evolution is possible without entirely unconventional ways of thinking, without the revolutionary spirit, without great sacrifices and discipline, without commitment, and without that most powerful and most daring set of emotions, which is called love.

The demagogues and propagandists of the Empire want us to believe that 'something ended'; they want us to accept defeat.

Why should we? There is no defeat anywhere on the horizon.

There are only two separate realities, two universes, into which our world had been shattered into: one of Western nihilism, another of revolutionary optimism.

***

I have already described the nihilism, but what do I imagine when I dream about that better, different world?

Do I envision red flags and people forming closed ranks, charging against some lavish palaces and stock exchanges? Do I hear loud revolutionary songs blasted from loudspeakers?

I actually do not. What comes to my mind is essentially very quiet and natural, human and warm.

There is a park near the old train station in the city of Granada, Nicaragua. I visited it some time ago. There, several old trees are throwing fantastic shadows on the ground, providing a desirable shade. Into a few big metal columns are engraved the most beautiful poems ever written in this country, while in between those columns stand simple but solid park benches. I sat on one of them. Not far from me, a couple of ageing lovers was holding hands, reading cheek to cheek from an open book. They were so close that they appeared to be forming a simple and totally self-sufficient universe. Above them were the shining verses written by Ernesto Cardenal, one of my favorite Latin American poets.

I also recall two Cuban doctors, sitting on a very different bench, thousands of miles away, chatting and laughing next to two goodhearted and corpulent nurses, after performing a complex surgery in Kiribati, an island nation 'lost' in the middle of South Pacific, a nation 'disappearing from the face of the earth because of global warming.

I remember many things, but they are never monumental, only warm and human. Because that is what revolution really is, I think: a couple of ageing peasants in a beautiful public park, both of them in love, holding hands, reading poetry to each other. It could also take form of two good-hearted doctors who travelled to the end of the world, just in order to save lives, far from the spotlight and fame.

And I always remember my dear friend, Eduardo Galeano, one of the greatest revolutionary writers of Latin America, telling me in Montevideo, about his eternal love for his wonderful lady called "Reality". Ms. Reality can often be as revolutionary as entire people's army.

Then I think: no, we cannot lose. We are not going to lose. The enemy is mighty and many people are weak and scared, but we will not allow the world to be converted into a mental asylum. We'll fight for each and every person who has been affected, and drowned in gloom.

We'll expose the abnormality and perversity of Western nihilism. We'll fight it with our revolutionary enthusiasm and optimism, and we will use the greatest weapons, such as poetry and love. And we will win, at the end we will win, although so many lives have been already lost, broken and devoured by the merciless Western nihilism.

April 1-5, 2017

London - Beirut

2
At Night I Hear Victims Screaming

It sometimes happens in the middle of a dark night, when I don't expect it, when I think that I am sound asleep but am not, or when perhaps I really am but not completely. I don't know. All that I witnessed and overheard, all that I thought I forgot but couldn't, all that I tried so desperately to forget comes back, first in spasms, then in full force.

I often think that the West went mad. Totally, irreversibly! It turned into a monster, and it keeps manufacturing new, smaller but equally toxic brutes all over the world. It rolls, smashing all that stands on its way. And I am not sure whether it still could be stopped.

Those horrid US military bases on

Kwajalein Atoll, Marshall Islands... those Israeli occupation forces choking the Syrian Golan Heights, those helicopter gunships firing at civilian vehicles in Gaza... bombed and burned villages near Mosul, Iraq... images of people slaughtered by pro-Western terrorists in Iran... men who were tortured savagely, and whose wives and daughters were brutally raped in "India-administered" Kashmir, clinging to each other desperately, whispering their stories in some godforsaken villages near the border with Pakistan.

Here, in this essay, I will not, and cannot go through the entire catalogue of horrors that has already penetrated my brain, deciding to stay with me, most likely, forever. The list is too long – almost endless.

Except that it's not just a list, but a mosaic of true events that occurred to hundreds and thousands of human being in all corners of the world, often in front of my own eyes.

Sometimes, in the middle of the night, I hear people screaming.

I try to work, write books and essays, and make films. I usually don't allow myself a luxury of talking to others about those nights.

But this time I will. Many of you asked what is fueling my writing; what keeps me going. And why do I dare doing what others don't, and going where almost no one goes.

Let me reply once and for all. Let me share at least a few personal moments with my readers.

I met a Syrian girl inside a small, informal and unnamed refugee camp, in Bekaa Valley, Lebanon, near the city of Zahlah. She was a immigrant, perhaps five or six years old. At first she was scared when I tried to take her photograph, but then she smiled. Eventually, she showed me her tongue, and moved it, cheekily, to one side of her mouth. She was standing there, in the middle of anonymous camp, with her older sister.

Then, a few moments later, she cautiously came closer to me and touched my hand.

Winter was approaching. Some refugees were freezing, and the girl was suffering from malnutrition. Her natural behavior, her innocence and her obvious oblivion of the war touched me tremendously.

A few weeks later, I drove back with sweets and toys. But the girl had already left. I was told that her family took her north to Aarsal, near the Syrian border where Hezbollah is locked in an epic battle with the ISIS. Yes, the same ISIS that were originally trained and armed by NATO in Turkey and Jordan.

I printed her photo and glued it to my refrigerator. I think about her often, almost every day. I don't know why.

In a way, her image, that of a simple girl, of a child standing in the middle of some horrid refugee camp near a war zone, is a symbol of insanity of the world in which we are forced to live.

In a way, she is a symbol of resistance against savagery of the Empire, a symbol of longing for something normal, longing for sanity in the middle of lunacy.

The conflict, the war in her country, Syria, is so "unnecessary", so bizarre, so obviously triggered by the West and its vile allies and interests.

Through her youth and eyes full of curiosity and hope, life was managing to prevail over death and dark destructive nihilism. But for how long could it last? In

Zahlah the girl was still winning, with her smile and her determination to live, to stay alive. But she is in Aarsal now, where war is ranging, mercilessly. I worry about her. I worry about her so much. And I curse the Empire.

Of course I saw plenty of things that could not be allowed to appear even on the pages of the publications with "tough", "hardened" readership. Some things were so horrible that they would break in half even someone as strong as a bull; things that should not have been seen by anyone, and especially happen to anyone.

Imagine a "refugee camp" near Goma, East Kivu, in the Democratic Republic of Congo (DRC), where an insane, stoned militia armed and supported by two closest allies of the West in the region – Rwanda and Uganda – had already raped almost all female inhabitants, from tiny babies to old grandmothers.

Imagine coltan and uranium and diamonds being smuggled from the DRC, shamelessly, under the direct supervision of the UN soldiers, so called "peacekeepers".

Imagine visiting several villages in Iraq,

near Mosul, villages that were first attacked by the ISIL and then bombed, mercilessly, by the USAF. Imagine that you have photographs, as you had photographs of those plundered and raped East Timor villages two decades ago, but frankly, nobody gives a fuck.

And you live with all this, day and night.

Say you saw several Palestinian men after being shot in their balls by Israeli soldiers. You have those images, too, from Shifa Hospital in Gaza. You have plenty of things like that, in your memory drives and in your head.

People without faces, people burned beyond recognition, still alive, still moving, still clinging to life.

It is an "all you can eat" medley of horrors and misery, brought to you by global capitalism, Western imperialism and cultural fundamentalism!

Then what do you do with it, at night?

When you are very young and see all this shit for the first time, you simply want to puke. And you puke, actually. Later, you stop puking and if you have balls or ovaries, you fight! You try to fight for much better world.

As time passes and most battles are becoming "uphill ones", you desperately want to be able to trust people or at least one person, one that had earlier came to you, offering to "share all this, and to fight by your side, forever". But your courage, as well as your dedication, outrage, zeal, desperation and longing gain you nothing, really. You are betrayed, again and again, perhaps because the stakes are too high, the burden too heavy, or simply because your life is actually excessively intense and totally different from the lives of other people.

The lonelier it gets, the more determined you become. There is no going back. The world is in flames. You know it. Not many others realize it. You understand how things are functioning. You have to fight; it is your duty and obligation. And you fight. But there are those nights...

You may be tough as a stone in the middle of terrible battlefields and other most horrendous situations, but at night, you are totally vulnerable and most likely alone.

"In a way, her image, that of a simple girl, of a child standing in the middle of some horrid refugee camp near a war zone, is a symbol of insanity of the world in which we are forced to live…"

When I reached the Eritrean port city of Massawa, almost one year ago, I felt thoroughly exhausted and burned out. I could hardly move, after working a few days earlier just a few kilometers from Mosul, Iraq, and right after that in Lebanon. I felt confused after being crushed and insulted by someone I trusted and fully relied on emotionally.

My Eritrean hosts got me a room in some old and terribly run down hotel.

Then, close to midnight, the electric generator gave up the ghost for the rest of the night. No one else was staying on my floor.

I clearly realized that real hell was ahead of me.

For 2 hours I was using the screen of my Mac Book Pro. After it went blank, my phone lasted a little bit longer. Then it was around 3:30AM and pitch dark.

The "procession" began.

I already described such situations in what will be, one day, my 1,000-page novel. But in my book, the victims are passing, night after night, through the secondary border post covered by deep snow, high in the mountains, between Argentina and Chile. They are passing on board old trucks, and in the morning, only deep holes in the virgin snow, holes created by warm streams of blood, could remain the main character about the events of the previous night.

In Eritrea, the victims of the Empire were passing only through in my mind, in my memory. They were passing one by one. Peruvian victims, Colombian victims; victims from Indonesia, Kashmir, Sri Lanka, Philippines, the DRC, Rwanda, Uganda, Kenya, Somalia, Iraq, Lebanon, Syria, Palestine, Turkey, Ivory Coast, Ukraine, Serbia, Nicaragua, Honduras... victims from dozens of other countries, mainly women; because women always suffer the most. Unnecessary deaths – people who just perished for no particular reason; only because the Empire could not stop looting, murdering, aiming at absolute control over the world.

At some point I gave up: I opened my eyes, staring into the darkness, fists clenched.

Everything inside the room was static. Only my memory was alive.

This was the price of knowing.

I was willing to pay anything; I was never known to be stingy. No price was too high for me.

Fighting against the Empire, exposing its barbarity, learning about its deeds – it all is tremendously overtaxing. Because the Empire is sick, because Western culture turned a long time ago into a pathology, because too many human beings are dying or are having their lives ruined, just so the excessive needs and appetites of the rulers of the world, of their global regime, are satisfied.

A few months after that dreadful night on the coast of Eritrea, I was invited to speak at the 14th International Symposium on the Contributions of Psychology to Peace, in Johannesburg and Pretoria, South Africa.

A few hours after delivering my presentation on the topic of absolute destruction of the African continent by Western imperialism, I found myself facing several top psychologists from all corners of the globe:

"How do you manage to survive all that you just described, psychologically and physically?"

I told them that I am not managing at all, but I have no choice. Someone has to do what I am doing. Otherwise no alternative, no real information could flow.

They asked me to take a break, to rest, for at least several months. I nodded. Then we all began to laugh. Psychologists are known to have a great sense of humour.

"I am absolutely devastated", my dear friend Binu Matthew, a legendary editor of the most important Indian left wing news site, *Countercurrents*, told me couple of months earlier, as we were driving through his state of Kerala. "I am coping with all those horrors that imperialism is spreading all over the world. It all goes through me. I suffer because of each piece of terrible information that is published by my site. It puts me through tremendous psychological strain."

When things get tough, I imagine a few people; men, women and children, from all corners of the world; people who touched me, who suffered immensely, and who are still most likely in distress.

Their faces, their tears, even their screams, motivate me to keep working.

The Syrian girl from a refugee camp in Bekaa Valley is one of them. I have no right to stop, to back down and to fail her.

It is tremendous shame, disgrace, the hard bottom that our civilization has managed to hit: profits over people, superiority dogmas, and above all – Western fascism.

But the battle is on.

My 1,000-page novel had been, for some time, delayed, but I incorporated many of its stories into my huge 820-page book, *Exposing Lies Of The Empire.*

One day, hopefully soon, humanism will win over dark nihilism; people will live for other people and not for some cold profits, religious dogmas and "Western values". Imperialism will be defeated once and for all.

One day we will be building enormous monuments to those who vanished, to those who suffered enormously, to "un-people" whose tears most of us do not even see, whose screams of horror and pain are muzzled by awful duvet of lies, by deranged pop music and movie soundtracks, by whoring mass media, and by a twisted formal education which is distributed to everyone like a poison, like sedatives, like a tool that makes most of the people on this scarred Earth disappear from our consciousness.

At night, I hear victims screaming, from pain, in agony. Therefore I fight, therefore I write, therefore I have no right to stop.

November 20, 2015

Andre Vltchek

3

The West is Manufacturing Muslim
Monsters

Who Should Be Blamed
For Muslim Terrorism?

A hundred years ago, it would have been unimaginable to have a pair of Muslim men enter a cafe or a public transportation vehicle, and then blow themselves up, killing dozens. Or to massacre the staff of a satirical magazine in Paris! Things like that were simply not done.

When you read the memoirs of Edward Said, or talk to old men and women in East Jerusalem, it becomes clear that the great part of Palestinian society used to be absolutely secular and moderate. It cared about life, culture, and even fashion, more than about religious dogmas.

The same could be said about many other Muslim societies, including those of Syria, Iraq, Iran, Egypt and Indonesia. Old photos speak for themselves. That is why it is so important to study old images again and again, carefully.

Islam is not only a religion; it is also an enormous culture, one of the greatest on Earth, which has enriched our humanity with some of the paramount scientific and architectural achievements, and with countless discoveries in the field of medicine. Muslims have written stunning poetry, and composed beautiful music. But above all, they developed some of the earliest social structures in the world, including enormous public hospitals and the first universities on earth, like The University of al-Qarawiyyin in Fez, Morocco.

The idea of 'social' was natural to many Muslim politicians, and had the West not brutally interfered, by overthrowing left-wing governments and putting on the throne fascist allies of London, Washington and Paris; almost all Muslim countries, including Iran, Egypt and Indonesia, would now most likely be socialist, under a group of very moderate and mostly secular leaders.

***

In the past, countless Muslim leaders stood up against the Western control of the world, and enormous figures like the Indonesian President, Ahmet Sukarno, were close to Communist Parties and ideologies. Sukarno even forged a global anti-imperialist movement, the Non-Allied movement, which was clearly defined during the Bandung Conference in Indonesia, in 1955.

That was in striking contrast to the conservative, elites-oriented Christianity, which mostly felt at home with the fascist rulers and colonialists, with the kings, traders and big business oligarchs.

For the Empire, the existence and popularity of progressive, Marxist, Muslim rulers governing the Middle East or resource-rich Indonesia, was something clearly unacceptable. If they were to use the natural wealth to improve the lives of their people, what was to be left for the Empire and its corporations? It had to be stopped by all means. Islam had to be divided, and infiltrated with extremists and anti-Communist cadres, and by those who couldn't care less about the welfare of their people.

***

Almost all radical rightwing movements in today's Islam, anywhere in the world, are tied to Wahhabism, an ultra-conservative, reactionary sect of Islam, which is in control of the political life of Saudi Arabia, Qatar and other staunch allies of the West in the Gulf.

To quote Dr. Abdullah Mohammad Sindi:

"It is very clear from the historical record that without British help neither Wahhabism nor the House of Saud would be in existence today. Wahhabism is a British-inspired fundamentalist movement in Islam. Through its defense of the House of Saud, the US also supports Wahhabism directly and indirectly regardless of the terrorist attacks of September 11, 2001. Wahhabism is violent, right wing, ultra-conservative,

> *rigid, extremist, reactionary, sexist, and intolerant..."*

The West gave full support to the Wahhabis in the 1980s. They were employed, financed and armed, after the Soviet Union was dragged into Afghanistan and into a bitter war that lasted from 1979 to 1989. As a result of this war, the Soviet Union collapsed, exhausted both economically and psychologically.

The Mujahedeen, who were fighting the Soviets as well as the left-leaning government in Kabul, were encouraged and financed by the West and its allies. This horrible conflict, totally manufactured by Washington, was the "Soviets' Vietnam", in the words of Zbigniew Brzezinski, its principal architect. The Muslim faithful came from all corners of the Islamic world, to fight a 'Holy War' against "Communist infidels."

According to the US Department of State archives:

> *"Contingents of so-called Afghan Arabs and foreign fighters who wished to wage jihad against the atheist communists. Notable among them was a young Saudi named Osama bin*

Laden, whose Arab group eventually evolved into al-Qaeda."

Muslim radical groups created and injected into various Muslim countries by the West included al-Qaeda, but also, more recently, ISIS (also known as ISIL). ISIS is an extremist army that was born in the 'refugee camps' on the Syrian/Turkish and Syrian/Jordanian borders, and which was financed by NATO and the West to fight the Syrian (secular) government of Bashar al-Assad.

Such radical implants have been serving several purposes. The West uses them as proxies in the wars it is fighting against its designated "enemies" – the countries that are still standing in the way to the Empire's complete domination of the world. Then, somewhere down the road, after these extremist armies 'get totally out of control' (and they always will), they can easily serve as scarecrows and as justification for the 'The War On Terror', or, like after ISIS took Mosul, as an excuse for the re-engagement of Western troops in Iraq.

Stories about the radical Muslim groups have constantly been paraded on the front pages of newspapers and magazines, or shown on television monitors, reminding readers 'how dangerous the world really is', 'how important Western engagement in it is', and consequently, how important surveillance is, how indispensable security measures are, as well as tremendous 'defense' budgets and wars against countless rogue states.

***

From a peaceful and creative civilization, that used to lean towards socialism, the Muslim nations and Islam itself, found itself to be suddenly derailed, tricked, outmaneuvered, infiltrated by foreign religious and ideological implants, and transformed by the Western ideologues and propagandists into one 'tremendous threat'; into the pinnacle and symbol of terrorism and intolerance.

The situation has been thoroughly grotesque, but nobody is really laughing – too many people have died as a result; too much has been destroyed!

Indonesia is one of the most striking historical examples of how such mechanisms of the destruction of progressive Muslim values really functions:

In the 1950s and early 1960s, the US, Australia and the West in general, were increasingly 'concerned' about the progressive anti-imperialist and internationalist stand of President Sukarno, and about the increasing popularity of the Communist Party of Indonesia (PKI). But they were even more anxious about the enlightened, socialist and moderate Indonesian brand of Islam, which was clearly allying itself with Communist ideals.

Christian anti-Communist ideologues and 'planners', including the notorious Jesuit Joop Beek, infiltrated Indonesia. They set up clandestine organizations there, from ideological to paramilitary ones, helping the West to plan the coup that in and after 1965 took between 1 and 3 million human lives.

Shaped in the West, the extremely effective anti-Communist and anti-intellectual propaganda spread by Joop Beek and his cohorts also helped to brainwash many members of large Muslim organizations, propelling them into joining the killing of Leftists, immediately after the coup. Little did they know that Islam, not only Communism, was chosen as the main target of the pro-Western, Christian 'fifth column' inside Indonesia, or more precisely, the target was the left-leaning, liberal Islam.

After the 1965 coup, the Western-sponsored fascist dictator, General Suharto, used Joop Beek as his main advisor. He also relied on Beek's 'students', ideologically. Economically, the regime related itself with mainly Christian business tycoons, including Liem Bian Kie.

In the most populous Muslim nation on earth, Indonesia, Muslims were sidelined, their 'unreliable' political parties banned during the dictatorship, and both the politics (covertly) and economy (overtly) fell under the strict control of a Christian, pro-Western minority. To this day, this minority has its complex and venomous net of anti-Communist warriors, closely-knit business cartels and mafias, media and 'educational outlets' including private religious schools, as well as corrupt religious preachers (many played a role in the 1965 massacres), and other collaborators with both the local and global regime.

Indonesian Islam has been reduced to a silent majority, mostly poor and without any significant influence. It only makes international headlines when its frustrated white-robed militants go trashing bars, or when its extremists, many related to the Mujahedeen and the Soviet-Afghan War, go blowing up nightclubs, hotels or restaurants in Bali and Jakarta.

Or do they even do that, really?

Former President of Indonesia and progressive Muslim cleric, Abdurrahman Wahid (forced out of office by the elites), once told me: "I know who blew up the Marriott Hotel in Jakarta. It was not an attack by the Islamists; it was done by the Indonesian secret services, in order to justify their existence and budget, and to please the West."

***

"I would argue that western imperialism has not so much forged an alliance with radical factions, as created them", I was told, in London, by my friend, and leading progressive Muslim intellectual, Ziauddin Sardar.

And Mr. Sardar continued:

"We need to realize that colonialism did much more than simply damage Muslim nations and cultures. It played a major part in the suppression and eventual disappearance of knowledge and learning, thought and creativity, from Muslim cultures. The colonial encounter began by appropriating the knowledge and learning of Islam, which became the basis of the 'European Renaissance' and 'the Enlightenment' and ended by eradicating this knowledge and learning from both Muslim societies and from history itself. It did that both by physical elimination – destroying and closing down institutions of learning, banning certain types of indigenous knowledge, killing off local thinkers and scholars – and by rewriting History as the history of western civilization into which all minor histories of other civilization are subsumed."

From the hopes of those post-WWII

years, to the total gloom of the present days – what a long and terrible journey it has been!

The Muslim world is now injured, humiliated and confused, almost always on the defensive.

It is misunderstood by the outsiders, and often even by its own people who are frequently forced to rely on Western and Christian views of the world.

What used to make the culture of Islam so attractive – tolerance, learning, concern for the wellbeing of the people – has been amputated from the Muslim realm, destroyed from abroad. What was left was only religion.

Now most of the Muslim countries are ruled by despots, by the military or corrupt cliques. All of them closely linked with the West and its global regime and interests.

As they did in several great nations and Empires of South and Central America, as well as Africa, Western invaders and colonizers managed to totally annihilate great Muslim cultures.

What forcefully replaced them were greed, corruption and brutality.

It appears that everything that is based

on different, non-Christian foundations is being reduced to dust by the Empire. Only the biggest and toughest cultures are still surviving.

Anytime a Muslim country tries to go back to its essence, to march its own, socialist or socially-oriented way – be it Iran, Egypt, Indonesia, or much more recently Iraq, Libya or Syria – it gets savagely demonized, tortured and destroyed.

The will of its people is unceremoniously broken, and democratically expressed choices overthrown.

For decades, Palestine has been denied freedom, as well as its basic human rights. Both Israel and the Empire spit at its right to self-determination. The Palestinian people are locked in a ghetto, humiliated, and murdered—with almost complete impunity. Religion is all that some of them have left.

The 'Arab Spring' was derailed and terminated almost everywhere, from Egypt to Bahrain, and the old regimes and military are back in power.

Like African people, Muslims in the Middle East and Asia are paying a terrible price for being born in countries rich in natural resources. But they are also brutalized for having, together with China, the greatest civilization in history, one that outshone all the cultures of the West.

***

Christianity looted and brutalized the world. Islam, with its great Sultans such as Saladin, stood against invaders, defending such marvelous cities as Aleppo and Damascus, Cairo and Jerusalem. But overall, it was more interested in building a just civilization, than in pillaging and wars.

Now hardly anyone in the West knows about Saladin or about the great scientific, artistic or social achievements of the Muslim world. But everybody is 'well informed' about the ISIS. Of course they know ISIS only as an 'Islamic extremist group', not as one of the main Western tools used to destabilize the Middle East.

As 'France is mourning' the deaths of the journalists at the offices of the satirical magazine, Charlie Hebdo (undeniably a terrible crime!), all over Europe it is again Islam which is being depicted as brutal and militant, not the West with its post-Crusade, Christian fundamentalist doctrines that keeps overthrowing and slaughtering all moderate, secular and progressive governments and systems in the Muslim world, leaving Muslim people at the mercy of deranged fanatics.

***

In the last five decades, around 10 million Muslims have been murdered because their countries did not serve the Empire, or did not serve it full-heartedly, or just were in the way. The victims were Indonesians, Iraqis, Algerians, Afghanis, Pakistanis, Iranians, Yemenis, Syrians, Lebanese, Egyptians, and the citizens of Mali, Somalia, Bahrain and many other countries. Some of their homelands have been turned to rubble.

The West identified the most horrible monsters, threw billions of dollars at them, armed them, gave them advanced military training, and then let them loose.

The countries that are breeding terrorism, Saudi Arabia and Qatar, are some of the closest allies of the West, and have never been punished for exporting horror all over the Muslim world and beyond. The kept Western media naturally never mentions such an obvious fact.

Impressive social Muslim movements like Hezbollah, which is presently engaged in mortal combat against the ISIS, but which also used to galvanize Lebanon during its fight against the Israeli invasion, are on the "terrorist lists" compiled by the West. It explains a lot, if anybody is willing to pay attention.

Seen from the Middle East, it appears that the West, just as during the crusades, is aiming at the absolute destruction of Muslim countries and Muslim culture.

As for the Muslim religion, the Empire only accepts the sheepish brands – those that accept extreme capitalism and the dominant global position of the West. The only other tolerable type of Islam is that which is manufactured by the West itself, and by its allies in the Gulf – designated to fight against all progress and social justice - the one that is devouring its own people.

January 9, 2015

4
Europe
Is Built on Corpses and
Plunder

(Speech given at the Chamber of Deputies of the Italian Parliament in Rome, on January 30, 2016)

Friends and Comrades, it is a great honor to be standing here – at the Chamber of Deputies of the Italian Parliament.

One year ago I was driving through the Bekaa Valley in Lebanon, monitoring the situation in the refugee camps there. Winter was approaching and the mountains on the Lebanese–Syrian border were covered by snow. It was cold, very cold.

Some 20 minutes after leaving Baalbek, I

spotted an extremely humble makeshift refugee camp, growing literally from the road, in the middle of nowhere.

I stopped. Together with my interpreter, I walked inside and engaged several people in conversation.

The situation was desperate. Children were hungry and could not register for schools through the UNHCR or through the Lebanese government, which, by that time, had almost collapsed. Many electronic food cards that were issued to the migrants did not function. Work permits were not offered, and without proper paperwork, local social services could not be used. In brief: a total disaster.

I was told that in this area, some Syrian migrants had already been starving.

This was Bekaa Valley, a tough place to start with, and full of ancient traditions, clans, gangs and narcotics-business. Refugees were expected to keep their heads down, or else...

Before I left, two little girls, two sisters, approached me. Both had swollen bellies, suffering from malnutrition. Both were dressed in rugs. Both looked deprived.

But after spotting my cameras, they

were mesmerized, smiling at me, showing tongues, laughing.

Their country was in ruins, their future uncertain.

But these were just two little girls in the middle of the mountains, two girls excited about each and every little detail of life. Such innocence! Such hope! People are people, and children are children, everywhere, even during wars.

Unfortunately, I have witnessed too many of them; too many wars. Too many barbarities performed by NATO, by the Empire, by the United States and Europe.

Later, working on the Greek island of Kos and in Calais in France, I kept thinking about those two girls, again and again.

The West (or call it NATO, or anything you like – we all know what I mean!) has, in the most cynical manner, destabilized and destroyed the entire Middle East. As it has in virtually all the continents of the world, it ruined tremendous cultures, plundered all it could put its hands on, turned proud people into slaves. Libya and Iraq are no more! I can testify, as I work all over the Middle East.

And then the West enclosed itself into

its gold-plated bunker, slowly and disgustingly digesting its booty!

How many refugees are there that Europe says: "it cannot accept"? 1 million? Tiny, miniscule Lebanon has 2 million, and it is coping; badly but coping!

And Lebanon did not destroy Syria, Libya, Afghanistan or Iraq.

You know how it all feels like? Like observing a woman who was gang-raped, whose husband was murdered in front of her own eyes, and whose beautiful house was looted. Now this woman, just in order to save her starving children from the rubbles, is forced to go to Europe, to the rapists and thieves who destroyed her life, asking for shelter and food. And they spit into her face! They say: "It is too much for us, too difficult to accommodate you and others like you! Woman, you came to take advantage of us. You came to have a better life at our expense!"

This is how it looks from the outside. This is how I see it.

And I want to puke. But there is no time... One has to work, day and night, to stop this madness.

The West, of course including Europe, is

too hardened by its own crimes, too cynical, and too unrepentant.

It remains blind, because it simply does not pay to see!

***

There is no Left Wing in Europe, anymore. Not the Left as we understand the term in Cuba and other revolutionary nations.

To us, true left means "Internationalism", solidarity!

True left is global, egalitarian, and color-blind.

The European so-called Left is only concerned with the benefits of its own citizens. It does not care at all where the funds are coming from.

As long as French, Greek, Spanish or Italian farmers get their subsidies and perks, who cares that agriculture in Africa or Asia gets thoroughly ruined. The most important is that European farmers could drive their latest BMW's, for producing something or not producing anything at all.

I saw absolutely grotesque concepts implemented in countries like Senegal, and other former French colonies: heavily subsidized French food produce flooded West Africa, supermarkets opened, local production collapsed. Then the prices spiked to 2-3 times higher levels than those in Paris. And so, in Senegal where incomes are perhaps only 10% of those in France, a yoghurt costs 3 times more than in *Monoprix.*

Who pays for those 35-hour workweeks? Who pays for socialized medical care and free education in the European Union? Definitely not the Europeans themselves! Most of the funds used to come from the colonies, from that unimaginable plunder of the world performed by the West.

Colonialism and imperialism are still there, but they often changed forms, although the toll on people in non-white countries continues to be the same.

The Belgian King Leopold II and his cohorts, in what is now Congo, massacred 10 million people, at the beginning of the 20th Century. Between 1995 and now, the West plundered the Democratic Republic of Congo once again, mercilessly, by using its closest allies in Africa – Rwanda, Uganda and Kenya. Again, between 7 and 10 million people died there, in just 20 years, and these are not some inflated numbers, these are numbers provided by the United Nations and its reports, including the so-called "Mapping Report". All that horror, only so the West could have access to coltan (used in our mobile phones), to uranium, and other strategic materials. I compiled the evidence in my feature documentary film "Rwanda Gambit".

All those ruined lives and countries, so that European citizens could have their benefits, long vacations, and social services.

When I discussed the issue with my friend, an Italian filmmaker from Naples, he snapped at me: "We don't want to be like the Chinese. We don't want to work hard like them!"

I replied: "Then live within your means! Do not allow your corporations and governments to massacre tens of millions of people, so that the companies could have their insane profits, and citizens those outrageous benefits."

Recently, in Thailand, I overheard a group of unemployed Spaniards laughing about having a vacation in Southeast Asia, paid for by their unemployment benefits.

I know many countries, dependencies of the West, where losing one's job is synonymous to a death sentence! But we are asked to feel sorry for Spaniards, Italians and Greeks. We are expected to see them as victims.

***

I am saddened to say, but it is not only the United States, but also Europe, which is totally, blissfully ignorant about its role in the world, and about the harm, about the horrors that it is spreading all over our Planet.

This discovery shocked me so much, that I spent 4 years crisscrossing the world, compiling the evidence and testimonies that illustrate the colonialist, neo-colonialist and imperialist legacy of the West, as well as the current neo-colonialist barbarities. The book is 840-pages long and it is called "Exposing Lies Of The Empire". I hope, one day, it will be available in the Italian language!

The book has been receiving enthusiastic reception, but for me, this thick volume is not the end. Now I am compiling the second installment. The topic is just too enormous. The crimes, genocides, holocausts committed by the West on the people of our Planet, are too enormous.

Everything is linked to them! The entire arrangement of the world uses them as pillars.

In our book "On Western Terrorism – From Hiroshima to Drone Warfare", written together with my friend Noam Chomsky, I was asked whether the Europeans actually realize what they have done to the world, during the last centuries.

(Just a side note – this book is now available in the Italian language "Terrorismo Occidentale").

I replied to Noam: "They definitely don't!"

And I repeat here, again: most of them, the great majority of them, do not realize it! They don't want to see, to admit, that their opera houses, hospitals, museums, parks and promenades, are all constructed on the corpses of those who were robbed of everything: from Latin America and its open veins, to Asia and Africa. Slavery, unimaginable extermination campaigns, tremendous lists of horrors!

Before Noam and I began our discussion, I spent some time with several top statisticians, and our conclusion was chilling: directly or indirectly, the West massacred between 40 and 50 million people, between the Hiroshima A-bomb explosion, and the time of my long dialogue with Noam – in 2012.

The number of people, who were murdered throughout history, directly or indirectly, by European empires, all over the world, can only be calculated in hundreds of millions, and one of my statistician friends believes that the total accumulative number actually exceeds 1 billion.

***

When I was recently speaking at the China Academy of Social Sciences in Beijing, and later in Moscow, having been invited by Russian philosophers and by several members of the Russian Academy of Science, I publicly declared that I am fundamentally against "free medical care and free education in Europe".

When asked "why?" I explained that the cost is too high, and those robbed and destroyed people, all over the world, are almost exclusively expected to cover it.

But I continued: "I am totally, decisively, supportive of universal free medical care, education and essential social benefits. Or as we say in Cuba: everyone dances, or nobody does!"

Of course I also can tolerate and support free medical care, education and benefits in those countries that do not plunder the world, like Cuba, China, Venezuela, Bolivia, South Africa or Ecuador.

***

Not only the West refuses to face its responsibility for, by now, the almost absolute total destruction of the world, it is also using all sorts of smoke screens and propaganda tactics to divert the attention of the people; it is spreading nihilist economic concepts, propaganda and outright lies.

It is using education as a weapon, offering scholarships to children of elites in the countries it is robbing and controlling. After being indoctrinated, they return home and continue violating their own countries on behalf of the United States and Europe.

And so the vicious cycle continues!

I encountered so many grotesque moments, when for instance, an Indonesian upper class family returning from its vacation in Holland, begins a long litany, about how great are the theaters, trains, museums and public spaces in Netherlands, compared to those in Indonesia.

Of course they are! All built from centuries of Dutch plunder of Indonesia, like those Spanish cathedrals stuffed with gold, growing from corpses.

As Noam Chomsky often says: "not to see all this truly takes great discipline!"

***

The brutality of the Western Empire is unmatchable. Its cynicism is monumental!

Look at those so-called "terrorists" in Muslim countries, scarecrows that Western governments and media keep waving in front of our eyes!

Islamic culture is greatly socialist and socially oriented. After World War II, secular, socialist, revolutionary and anti-Western governments ruled the most important Muslim nations: Egypt, Iran and Indonesia.

Within two decades, the West overthrew them all, implementing fascist regimes.

It then invented the *Mujahideen* and injected them into Afghanistan, in order to finish with the Soviet Union.

And once it felt the need for some monumental enemy to replace Communism, it manufactured and then armed, trained and educated groups like al-Qaida, al-Nusra and ISIS.

This move served two important goals: to justify astronomical military and intelligence budgets, and to portray the Western/Christian civilization as "culturally superior", fighting "Arab terrorist monsters".

Of course, the great majority of the people in Europe and North America are so indoctrinated, intellectually self-righteous and defunct, that they remain blind when faced with those Machiavellian pirouettes.

For the European public, there are plenty of "good reasons" to stick to those inherently racist beliefs, and to protectionism. There are even better reasons for hiding those millions of heads in the sand!

And so it goes.

***

I am here, in Italy, and today I do not want to discuss the United States, Israel, or other colonies and client states of the West. We can do it some other time, if I am invited back.

I spoke about Europe.

And I spoke about those two Syrian girls I met in Lebanon.

They are your responsibility, too, Italy! They suffer from malnutrition because your part of the world is ruining their country. It is because your country is a member of NATO, and NATO is behaving like a fascist thug with some clear mafia behavioral patterns.

I know you have heart!

I grew up on you films, on Fellini and de Sica, Rossellini, Antonioni and others. I greatly admire your poetry and music. They had tremendous influence on my work, and on how I see the world.

But your heart, it seems, lately goes only to your own people. It is not an internationalist heart. It does not believe that all people are equal.

I came here to say this, because not too many people dare to.

I came here because I still care for your country.

But as a determined socialist realist, I care about Italy as it "could and should be", not "as it is" at this moment.

Thank you!

January 30, 2016

Andre Vltchek

5
Academia: Hands off Revolutionary Philosophy!

Philosophers have been muzzled by the Western global regime; most of great modern philosophy concealed from the masses. What has been left of it, allowed to float on the surface is toothless, irrelevant and incomprehensible: a foolish outdated theoretical field for those few remaining intellectual snobs.

Philosophy used to be the most precious crown jewel of human intellectual achievement. It stood at the vanguard of almost all fights for a better world. Gramsci was a philosopher, and so were Lenin, Mao Tse-tung, Ho-Chi-Minh, Guevara, Castro, Frantz Fanon, Senghors, Cabral, Nyerere and Lumumba, to name just a few.

To be a thinker, a philosopher, in ancient China, Japan or even in some parts of the West, was the most respected human 'occupation'.

In all 'normally' developing societies, knowledge has been valued much higher than material possessions or naked power.

In ancient Greece and China, people were able to understand the majority of their philosophers. There was nothing "exclusive" in the desire to know and interpret the world. Philosophers spoke to the people, for the people.

Some still do. But that whoring and servile Western academic gang, which has locked philosophy behind the university walls, viciously sidelines such men and women.

Instead of leading people to the barricades, instead of addressing the most urgent issues our world is now facing, official philosophers are fighting amongst themselves for tenures, offering their brains and bodies to the Empire. At best, they are endlessly recycling each other, spoiling millions of pages of paper with footnotes, comparing conclusions made by

Derrida and Nietzsche, hopelessly stuck at exhausted ideas of Kant and Hegel.

At worst, they are outrightly evil – making still relevant revolutionary philosophical concepts totally incomprehensible, attacking them, and even disappearing them from the face of the Earth.

***

Only the official breed, consisting of almost exclusively white/Western 'thought recyclers', is now awarded the right to be called 'philosophers'.

My friends in all corners of the world, some of the brightest people on earth, are never defined as such. The word 'philosopher' still carries at least some great theoretical prestige, and god forbid if those who are now fighting against Western terror, for social justice or true freedom of thought, were to be labeled as such!

But they are, of course, all great philosophers! And they don't recycle – they go forward, advancing brilliant new concepts that can improve life on our

Planet. Some have fallen, some are still alive, and some are still relatively young:

Eduardo Galeano – one of the greatest storytellers of all times, and a dedicated fighter against Western imperialism. Noam Chomsky – renowned linguist and relentless fighter against Western fascism. Pramoedya Ananta Toer – former prisoner of conscience in Suharto's camps and the greatest novelist of Southeast Asia. John Steppling – brilliant American playwright and thinker. Christopher Black – Canadian international lawyer and fighter against illegal neo-colonialist concepts of the Empire. Peter Koenig – renowned economist and thinker. Milan Kohout, thinker and performer, fighter against European racism.

Yes – all these great thinkers; all of them, philosophers! And many more that I know and love – in Africa and Latin America and Asia especially…

For those who insist that in order to be called a philosopher, one has to be equipped with some stamp that shows that the person has passed a test and is allowed to serve the Empire, here is proof to the contrary:

Even according to the Dictionary of Modern American philosophers (online ed.). New York: Oxford University Press:

"The label of "philosopher" has been broadly applied in this Dictionary to intellectuals who have made philosophical contributions regardless of academic career or professional title. The wide scope of philosophical activity across the time-span of this Dictionary would now be classed among the various humanities and social sciences which gradually separated from philosophy over the last one hundred and fifty years. Many figures included were not academic philosophers but did work at philosophical foundations of such fields as pedagogy, rhetoric, the arts, history, politics, economics, sociology, psychology, linguistics, anthropology, religion, and theology."

***

In his brilliant upcoming book *Aesthetic Resistance and Dis-Interest*, my friend John Steppling quotes, Hullot-Kentor:

"If art – when art is art – understands us better than we can intentionally understand ourselves, then a philosophy of art would

need to comprehend what understands us. Thinking would need to become critically imminent to that object; subjectivity would become the capacity of its object, not simply its manipulation. That's the center of Adorno's aesthetics. It's an idea of thought that is considerably different from the sense of contemporary "theory", where everyone feels urged to compare Derrida with Nietzsche, the two of them with Levinas, and all of them now with Badiou, Žižek and Agamben. That kind of thinking is primarily manipulation. It's the bureaucratic mind unconsciously flexing the form of social control it has internalized and wants to turn on others."

Western academia is rigidly defining, which lines of thought are acceptable for philosophers to use, as well as what analyses, and what forms.

Those who refuse to comply are 'not true philosophers'. They are dilettantes, 'amateurs'.

And those who are not embraced by some 'reputable' institution are not to be taken seriously at all (especially if they are carrying Russian, Asian, African, Middle Eastern or Latino names). It is a little bit like with journalism. Unless you have an 'important' media outlet behind you (preferably a Western one), unless you can show that the Empire truly trusts you, your press card is worth nothing, and you would not even be allowed to board a UN or a military flight to a war zone.

Your readers, even if numbering millions, may see you as an important philosopher. But let's be frank: unless the Empire stamps its seal of acceptance on your forehead or backside, in the West you are really nothing more than some worthless shit!

***

BLURRING THE WORK OF REVOLUTIONARY PHILOSOPHERS

After all that I have witnessed and written, I am increasingly convinced that Western imperialism and neo-colonialism are the most urgent and dangerous challenges facing our Planet. Perhaps the only challenges...

I have seen 180 countries and territories in all corners of the Globe. I have witnessed wars, conflicts, imperialist theft and indescribable brutality of white tyrants.

And so, recently, I sensed that it is time to revisit two great thinkers of the 20th Century, two determined fighters against Western imperialist fascism: Frantz Fanon and Jean-Paul Sartre.

The Wretched of the Earth, and ***Black Skin, White Masks*** – two essential books by Frantz Omar Fanon, a Martinique-born Afro-Caribbean psychiatrist, philosopher, revolutionary, and writer, and a dedicated fighter against Western colonialism. And *Colonialism and Neocolonialism*, a still greatly relevant book by Jean-Paul Sartre, a prominent French resistance fighter, philosopher, playwright and novelist...

I had all three books in my library and, after many years, it was time to read them again.

But my English edition of *Colonialism and Neocolonialism* was wrapped in dozens of pages of prefaces and introductions. The 'intellectual cushioning' was too thick and at some point I lost interest, leaving the book in Japan. Then in Kerala I picked up another, this time Indian edition.

Again, some 60 pages of prefaces and

introductions, pre-chewed intrusive and patronizing explanations of how I am supposed to perceive both Sartre and his interactions with Fanon, Memmi and others. And yes, it all suddenly began moving again into that pre-chewed but still indigestible "Derrida-Nietzsche" swamp.

Instead of evoking outrage and wrath, instead of inspiring me into taking concrete revolutionary action, those prefaces, back covers, introductions and comments were clearly castrating and choking the great messages of both Sartre and Fanon. They were preventing readers and fellow philosophers from getting to the core.

Then finally, when reaching the real text of Sartre, it all becomes clear – why exactly is the regime so determined to "protect" readers from the original writing.

It is because the core, the original, is extremely simple and powerful. The words are relevant, and easy to understand. They are describing both old French colonialist barbarities, as the current Western neo-colonialism. God forbid someone puts two and two together!

Philosopher Sartre on China and Western fascist cultural propaganda:

"As a child, I was a victim of the picturesque: everything had been done to make the Chinese intimidating. I was told about rotten eggs... of men sawn between two planks of wood, of piping and discordant music... [The Chinese] were tiny and terrible, slipping between your fingers, attacked from behind, burst out suddenly in a ridiculous din... There was also the Chinese soul, which I was simply told was inscrutable. 'Orientals, you see...' The Negroes did not worry me; I had been taught that they were good dogs. With them, we were still among mammals. But the Asians frightened me..."

Sartre on Western colonialism and racism:

"Racism is inscribed in the events themselves, in the institutions, in the nature of the exchange and the production. The political and social statuses reinforce one another: since the natives are sub-human, the Declaration of Human Rights does not apply to them; conversely, since they have no rights, they are abandoned without protection to the inhuman forces of nature, to the 'iron laws' of economics..."

And Sartre goes further:

"Western humanism and rights discourse

had worked by excluding a majority of the world's population from the category of humans."

I address the same issues and so are Chomsky, Cobb, Roy and others. But the Empire does not want people to know that Sartre, Memmi and Fanon spoke 'the same language' as we do, already more than half a century ago!

Albert Memmi:

"Conservatism engenders the selection of mediocre people. How can this elite of usurpers, conscious of their mediocrity, justify their privileges? Only one way: diminish the colonized in order to exult themselves, deny the status of human beings to the natives, and deprive them of basic rights..."

Sartre on Western ignorance:

"It is not cynicism, it is not hatred that is demoralizing us: no, it is only the state of false ignorance in which we are made to live and which we ourselves contribute to maintaining..."

The way the West 'educates' the world, Sartre again:

"The European elite set about fabricating a native elite; they selected adolescents,

marked on their foreheads, with a branding iron, the principles of Western culture, stuffed into their mouths verbal gags, grand turgid words which stuck to their teeth; after a brief stay in the mother country, they were sent back, interfered with..."

***

It is actually easy to learn how to recycle the thoughts of others, how to compare them and at the end, how to compile footnotes. It takes time, it is boring, tedious and generally useless, but not really too difficult. Academics could be easily 'manufactured', and they are.

On the other hand, it is difficult to create brand new concepts, to revolutionize the way our societies, and our world are arranged. If our brains recycle too much and try to create too little, they get lazy and sclerotic – chronically sclerotic.

Intellectual servility is a degenerative disease.

Western art has deteriorated to ugly psychedelic beats, to excessively bright colors and infantile geometric drawings, to cartoons and nightmarish and violent films as well as "fiction". It is all very convenient – with all that noise, one cannot hear anymore the screams of the victims, one cannot understand loneliness, and comprehend emptiness.

In bookstores, all over the world (except in some Latin American countries), poetry and philosophy sections are shrinking or outright disappearing.

Now what? Is it going to be Althusser (mostly not even real Althusser, but a recycled and abbreviated one), or Lévi-Strauss or Derrida, each wrapped in endless litanies of academic talk?

No! Comrades, philosophers, not that! Down with the sclerotic, whoring academia and their interpretation of philosophy!

Down with the assassins of Philosophy!

Philosophy is supposed to be the intellectual vanguard. It is synonymous with revolution, humanism, and rebellion.

Those who are thinking about and fighting for a much better world, using their brains as weapons, are true philosophers.

Those who are collecting dust, PhDs and tenures in some profit-oriented institutions of higher 'learning' are definitely not, even if they have hundreds of diplomas and stamps all over their walls, foreheads and buttocks!

They do not create and do not lead. They do not even teach! They are muzzling knowledge. To quote Fanon: "Everything can be explained to the people, on the single condition that you want them to understand." But "they" don't want people to understand; they really don't...

And one more thing: the great thoughts of Fanon and Sartre, of Gramsci and Mao, Guevara and Galeano should be gently washed, undusted and exhibited again, free of all those choking 'analyses' and comparisons compiled by toxic pro-establishment thinkers.

There is nothing to add to the writing of maverick revolutionary philosophers. Hands off their work! Let them speak! Editions without prefaces and introductions, please; no footnotes! The greatest works of philosophy were written with heart, blood and passion! No interpretation is needed. If allowed to read them, even a child can understand.

February 29, 2016

6
Why I Am
a Communist!

There are several essential messages literally shouting from the screen, whenever one watches 'The Last Supper' (La Ultima Cena), a brilliant 1976 film by a Cuban director Tomas Gutierrez Alea.

The utmost one: it is impossible to enslave an entire group or race of people, at least not indefinitely. Longing for freedom, for true liberty, is impossible to break, no matter how brutally and persistently colonialism, imperialism, racism and religious terror try to.

The second, equally important message is that the whites and the Christians (but mostly the white Christians) have been behaving, for centuries and all over the world, like a horde of savage beasts and

83

genocidal maniacs.

At the end of April 2016, on board *Cubana de Aviacion* jet that was taking me from Paris to Havana, I couldn't resist opening my computer and watching *La Ultima Cena* again, for at least the tenth time in my life.

Gutierrez on my screen, *Granma Internacional* (official Cuban newspaper named after the boat which brought Fidel, "Che" and other revolutionaries to Cuba, triggering the Revolution) and a glass of pure and honest rum on my table, I felt at home, safe and blissfully happy. After several depressing days in Paris, I was finally leaving that gray, increasingly gloomy, oppressive and self-righteous Europe behind.

Latin America was waiting for me. It was facing terrible attacks organized by the West. Its future was once again uncertain. "Our governments" were bleeding, some of them collapsing. The appalling extreme right-wing government of Mauricio Macri in Argentina has been busy dismantling the social state. Brazil was suffering from the political coup performed by corrupt right-wing lawmakers. Venezuela's Bolivarian

Revolution was struggling, literally fighting for its survival. Treasonous reactionary forces were confronting both Ecuador and Bolivia.

I was asked to come. I was told: "Latin America needs you. We are fighting a war for survival". And here I was, on board the *Cubana*, going 'home', to the part of the world that has always been so dear to me, and has shaped me into what I am now, as a man and as a writer.

I was going 'home', because I wanted to, but also because it was my duty. And I damn believe in duties!

After all, I'm not an anarchist but a Communist, 'educated' and hardened in Latin America.

***

But what does it mean when I say: 'I'm a Communist?'

Am I a Leninist, a Maoist, or a Trotskyist? Do I subscribe to the Soviet or the Chinese model?

Honestly, I have no idea! Frankly, I don't care much for those nuances.

To me personally, a true Communist is a fighter against imperialism, racism, 'Western exceptionism', colonialism and neo-colonialism. Yes, he or she is a determined Internationalist, a person who believes in equality and social justice for all people on this Earth.

I'll leave theoretical discussions to those who have plenty of time on their hands. I never even re-read the entire *Das Kapital*. It is too long. I read it when I was 16 years old. I think that reading it once is enough, even more than enough... It's not the only pillar of Communism and it is not some holy scripture that should be constantly quoted.

More than *Das Kapital*, I was influenced by what I saw in Africa, the Middle East, Asia and Latin America. I saw the entire world, some 180 countries and territories; I lived on all continents. Wherever I went, I witnessed the horrors of ongoing Western plunder of the Planet.

I saw the Empire forcing countries into bestial civil wars; wars sparked so the multi-national companies could comfortably loot. I saw millions of refugees from once proud and wealthy (or from potentially wealthy) countries that were ruined by the West: Congolese refugees, Somali refugees, Libyan and Syrian refugees, and refugees from Afghanistan... I saw inhuman conditions in factories that looked like purgatories; I saw monstrous sweatshops, mines, and fields near feudally run villages. I saw hamlets and townships, where the entire population vanished – dead from hunger, diseases, or both.

I also spent days and days listening to shocking testimonies of victims of torture. I spoke to mothers who lost their children, to wives who lost husbands, to husbands whose wives and daughters were raped in front of their eyes.

And the more I saw, the more I witnessed, the more shocking the stories I heard; the more obliged I felt to take sides, to fight for what I believe could be a much better world.

I wrote two books compiling hundreds of stories of terror committed by the West: "Exposing Lies Of The Empire" and "Fighting Against Western Imperialism".

It didn't bother me how derogatorily the Empire has been in depicting people who are still faithful to their ideals; ready to sacrifice everything, or almost everything, for the struggle against injustice.

I'm not afraid of being ridiculed. But I am terrified of wasting my life if I put selfishness on a pedestal, elevating it above the most essential humanistic values.

I believe that a writer cannot be 'neutral' or apolitical. If he is, then he is a coward. Or he is a liar.

Naturally, some of the greatest modern writers were or are Communists: Jose Saramago, Eduardo Galeano, Pablo Neruda, Mo Yan, Dario Fo, Maxim Gorki, Gabriel Garcia Marquez, to name just a few. Not a bad company, not bad at all!

And I believe that living and struggling for others is much more fulfilling than living only for one's own selfish interests and pleasures.

***

I admire Cuba for what it has done for humanity, in almost six decades of its revolutionary existence. Cuban Internationalism is what I personally see as 'my Communism'.

Cuba has heart and it has guts. It knows how to fight, how to embrace, how to sing and dance and how not to betray its ideals.

Is Cuba ideal? Is it perfect? No, of course it is not. But I don't demand perfection, from countries or from people, or from the Revolutions for that matter. My own life is very far from 'perfect'. We all make errors and bad decisions: countries, people as well as movements.

Perfection actually horrifies me. It is cold, sterile and self-righteous. It is ascetic, puritanical, and therefore inhuman, even perverse. I don't believe in saints. And I feel embarrassed when someone pretends to be one. Those small errors and 'imperfections' are actually making people and countries so warm, so lovable, so human.

The general course of the Cuban Revolution has never been 'perfect', but it has always been based on the deepest, most essential roots of humanism. And even when Cuba stood for some short time alone, or almost alone (it was China at the end, as I wrote and as Fidel shortly after confirmed in his "Reflections", that extended to Cuba its mighty fraternal hand) – it bled, it suffered and shivered from pain brought by countless betrayals, but it did not stir from its path, it did not kneel, it did not beg and it never surrendered!

This is how I think people and countries should live. They should not exchange ideals for trinkets, love for security and advantages, decency for cynical and bloodstained rewards. *Patria no se vende*, they say in Cuba. Translated loosely: 'The Fatherland should never be sold'. I also believe that Humanity should never be sold, as well as Love.

And that is why I am a Communist!

***

Betraying what we – human beings – really are, as well as betraying the poorest of the poor and the most vulnerable among us is, I believe, more frightening than suicide, than death.

A person, a country or a culture that thrives on the suffering of others, is defunct, thoroughly immoral.

The West had been doing exactly that, for decades and centuries. It has been living from and thriving on the enslavement of others and usurping everything on and under the surface of our Earth. It has corrupted, morally and financially, millions of people in its colonies and client states, turning them into shameless and spineless collaborators. It has 'educated', indoctrinated and organized huge armies of traitors, on all continents, in almost all corners of the world.

Forcing people to betrayal is the most powerful weapon of the Western Empire – forcing them to betrayal and oblivion.

The West turns human beings into prostitutes and butlers, and those who refuse, into prisoners and martyrs.

Indoctrination is well planned. Dreams are poisoned and ideals dragged through dirt. Nothing pure is allowed to survive.

People are made to fantasize only about hardware; phones and tablets, cars and television sets, diplomas. But the messages are empty, full of nihilism, repetitive and shallow. Cars can now drive very fast, but there is nothing really significant waiting at the end of the journey. Phones have thousands of functions and applications, but they are broadcasting increasingly trivial messages. "High definition" and sleek television sets are regurgitating propaganda and intellectually toxic entertainment.

It all brings profits to big corporations. It guarantees obedience. It strengthens the regime. But in many ways, humanity is getting poorer and poorer, while the Planet is almost entirely ruined.

Beauty is replaced with images full of gore. Knowledge is spat on, substituted by primitive pop and controlled academic "achievements". It is confused with those official-looking diplomas and stamps of approval issued by the indoctrination centers called universities: "Graduated: ready to serve the Empire!"

Poetry is gone, from most of bookstores, and from life.

Love is now shaped on pop culture images, anchored in some 'retro', oppressive and outdated religious dogmas.

It is clear that only Communism has so far been strong enough to confront the essence of the mightiest and the most destructive forces on our Planet: Western colonialism/ imperialism, which is locked in a disgusting and incestuous marriage with its own offspring – cruel feudal, capitalist and religious gangs of 'local elites' in conquered and ruined countries all over the world.

Both the Empire and its servants are betraying humanity. They are ruining the Planet, pushing it into the state where it could soon become uninhabitable. Or where life itself could lose all its meaning.

To me, to be a true Communist means this: to be engaged in the constant fight against the incessant rape of human brains, bodies and dignity, against the plunder of resources and nature, against selfishness and consequent intellectual and emotional emptiness.

I don't care under which flag it is done – red with the hammer and sickle, or red with several yellow stars. I'm fine with either of them, as long as the people holding those banners are honest and concerned with the fate of humanity and our Planet.

And as long as people calling themselves Communists are still able to dream and to fight!

***

Western propagandists tell you: "show us one perfect Communist society!"

I answer: "There is no such society. Human beings, as we have determined, are incapable of creating anything perfect. Fortunately!" Only religious fanatics are aiming at 'perfection'. Humans would die of boredom in a perfect world.

Revolution, a Communist Revolution, is a journey; it is a process. It is a huge, heroic attempt to build a much better world, using human brains, muscles, hearts, poetry and courage! It is a perpetual process, where people give more than they take, and when there is no sacrifice, only a fulfillment of duty towards humankind.

'Che' Guevara once said: "Sacrifices made should not be displayed as some identity card. They are nothing less than fulfilled obligations."

Maybe in the West, it is too late for such concepts to flourish. Selfishness, cynicism, greed and indifference have been successfully injected into the sub-consciousness of the majority of people. Perhaps that is why, despite all those material and social privileges, the inhabitants of Europe and North America (but also of Japan) appear to be so depressed and gloomy. They live only for themselves, at the expense of others. They want more and more material goods and more and more privileges.

They have lost the ability to define their own condition, but probably, deep inside, they feel emptiness, intuitively sensing that something is terribly wrong.

And that's why they hate Communism. That's why they stick to self-righteous lies, deceptions and dogmas delivered to them by the regime's propaganda. If Communists were right, then they would be wrong. And they suspect that they may be wrong. Communism is their bad conscience, and it brings fear that the bubble of deceptions could one day get exposed.

Most people in the West, even those who claim that they belong to the Left, want Communism to go away. They want to smear it, cover it with filth; bring it 'to their level'. They want to muzzle it. They are desperately trying to convince themselves that Communism is wrong. Otherwise, the responsibility for the hundreds of millions of lost lives would haunt them incessantly. Otherwise, they would have to hear and maybe even accept that the privileges of Europeans and North Americans are constructed on dreadful crimes against humanity! Otherwise, they would be forced to, on moral grounds, dismantle those privileges (something truly unthinkable, given the mindset of Western culture).

The recent position of the majority of Europeans towards the refugees coming from countries destabilized by the West, clearly shows how morally defunct the West really is. It is incapable of basic ethical judgments. Its ability to think logically has collapsed.

But the West is still ruling the world. Or more precisely, it is twisting its arm, pushing it towards disaster.

Western imperialist logic is simple: "If we rape and loot, it is because if we don't, others would! Everybody is the same. It cannot be helped. What we do is essential to human nature."

It is not. It is rubbish. I have seen people behaving better, much better than that, almost everywhere outside the Western world and its colonies. Even when they manage to slip away from their torturers and jailers – the Empire – for only a few years, they behave much better. But usually they are not allowed to slip away for too long: the Empire hits powerfully against those who dare to dream about freedom. It arranges coups against rebellious governments, destabilizes economies, supports the 'opposition', or directly invades.

It is absolutely clear to anyone who is still able and willing to see, that if the criminal Western Empire collapses, human beings would want to, they'd be capable of building great egalitarian and compassionate societies.

I believe that this is not the end. People are waking up from indoctrination, from stupor.

New, powerful anti-imperialist alliances are being forged. The year 2016 is not 1996 when there seemed to be almost no hopes left.

The war is waged, the war for the survival of humankind.

It is not a classical war of bullets and missiles. It is a war of nerves and ideals, dreams and information.

Before passing away, the great Uruguayan writer and revolutionary, Eduardo Galeano, told me: "Soon the time will come, and the world will erect old banners again!"

It is happening now! In Latin America, Africa and Asia, in almost all parts of the former Soviet Union and in China, people are demanding more Communism, not less. They don't always call Communism by its name, but they are crying for its essence: freedom and solidarity, passion, fervor, courage to change the world, equality, justice and internationalism.

I have no doubt that we will win. But I also suspect that before we do, the Empire will bathe entire continents in blood. Desire of Westerners to rule and to control is pathological. They are ready to murder millions of those who are unwilling to fall on their knees. They already murdered hundreds of millions, throughout the centuries. And they will sacrifice millions more.

But this time, they will be stopped.

I believe it, and shoulder-to-shoulder with others, I am working day and night to make it happen.

Because it is my duty…
Because I'm a Communist!

May 16, 2016

Andre Vltchek

7
Western Propaganda – So Simple But So Effective!

When some time ago Noam Chomsky and I met at MIT, in order to write a book together ("On Western Terrorism: From Hiroshima to Drone Warfare") and to produce a film with the same title, the topic we mainly aimed at discussing was that of the countless genocides the West has committed all over the world since the end of the WWII. The second topic was impunity.

But no matter what atrocities we re-visited during our dialogue, our conversation kept slipping towards one crucial theme: the propaganda that has been manufactured in mass media centers

101

like New York, Paris, London and other North American and European cities; the propaganda created in order to twist both the past and the present. Without such brainwashing and the almost total indoctrination of the Western general public and the 'elites' in all of the 'client' states, no imperialist and neo-colonialist policies would have become truly successful—or even possible.

We spoke about US commercial advertising and its influence on German Nazi propaganda, and about Nazi propaganda methods influencing both the US and European propaganda-makers. Noam kept asking me about my childhood in socialist Czechoslovakia, and I explained to him, honestly, how indoctrinated I was as a teenager: not by the Communist dogmas, but by the BBC, the Voice of America and the Radio Free Europe – all of them relentlessly spreading the Western political and market gospel to all corners of the socialist world.

Both Noam and I have written dozens of essays on the topic, as well as several books. My latest one, covering all the corners of the world where the Empire is spreading destruction, followed by indoctrination, has more than 800 pages, and is called "Exposing Lies of the Empire".

And I always feel that even this massive book just touches the tip of the iceberg, that it is only a beginning!

Western propaganda is actually a perfect apparatus. It is effective and it is almost fully 'bulletproof'. It 'works'!

European empires have been refining it for many long centuries, and the European offspring – the United States – has brought it to almost total perfection.

One precondition for its success is, of course, that the Western political and economic regime owns almost all the major media channels and distribution outlets of the world. Diversity can never be tolerated, because it could smash the idiocy!

Once this prerequisite is completed, things get relatively relaxed and cozy for the demagogues in Washington, London and Paris. Unopposed and unchallenged, they can attack anybody or anything, without fear and consequences.

***

Here is just an example of how easy it is to smear a world leader who resists the imperialist designs of the Empire:

Imagine that one sunny morning, some 10 major newspapers and television stations declare that various anonymous but highly reliable sources in Moscow have informed them that the Russian President Vladimir Putin is a vampire!

This 'news' would fly all over the world. Many readers and viewers would at first roll around on the floor laughing, but some would not. And even several of those who found the information thoroughly bizarre and unbelievable would at some point realize that seeds of doubt were beginning to grow inside their brains: "OK, it is absurd, of course, but what if? What if? How awful that would be!"

But how can one really prove that he or she is not a vampire? Or how can one prove that he or she has not been visited and corrupted by some evil extra-terrestrial flying saucers, at least on several occasions?

At some point, the Russian President would feel that he had enough of the charade. He'd go to the best university clinic in Moscow, and ask for a certificate that clearly stated that he is not a vampire.

Several leading academics and doctors would get involved and produce a complex and thoroughly scientific conclusion, which would resolutely declare that President of the Russian Federation – Vladimir Putin - is not a vampire.

Shocked by and reacting to the vulgarity demonstrated by the Western propaganda tsars, most of the Russian media outlets would offer some commonsense and logic: "Can't we all see clearly that he cannot be a vampire? All his teeth are of approximately equal length, he socializes during the day, he does not sleep in a coffin, he eats garlic and he is not scared of crosses; be they Orthodox, Protestant or Catholic ones!"

Others would argue that there are actually no real vampires inhabiting our Planet.

This is when the Western mass media would go into overdrive. Sarcastically it would declare that the Russian academia, Russian doctors and Russian media cannot be trusted – they are all under the heel of the state, and on top of it they have been infiltrated by the nation's secret services and former KGB agents.

"And doesn't 'Vlad' sound somehow similar to 'Bran', which is the castle in Romania, which in turn used to be the home base of the commander-in-chief of all militant vampires – Count Dracula?"

There would still be some rational resistance: "No, 'Vlad' does not really sound like 'Bran', and anyway, nobody in Russia calls Mr. Putin 'Vlad' – only the Western media does, in clearly derogatory way."

But such voices of reason would almost never reach the general public all over the world!

And on it goes.

In the end, a few billions of human brains would register and subconsciously store the 'vampire theory', and they would never again look at the President of Russia, or at his country, with the same eyes!

Of course the Russian leadership is not the only one that the West is targeting.

There is a relentless flow of 'shocking' rumors and derogatory remarks made by the mainstream media against the President of China, of Byelorussia, against the leadership of Iran, South Africa, Eritrea, Zimbabwe, Syria, and North Korea, as well as against all the left-wing governments of Latin America.

After being repeated hundreds of times, the rumors, at least for many people, get confused with facts, and then get accepted as facts.

When still leading Cuba, Fidel Castro was constantly 'dying' or 'disappearing'. The North Korean government has been relentlessly portrayed as a desperate gang of bloodthirsty sexual maniacs, executing and raping almost everything that moves. The ANC and especially President Zuma have done 'nothing to close that staggering social divide in South Africa'. In South America, the pro-Western media outlets invented and then perfected a new lucrative industry: manufacturing corruption scandals and implicating in them virtually all of the popular socialist leaders.

Nihilism, darkest 'news' and scenarios have been force-fed to the public, in order to eradicate all the zeal and optimism that comes from the countries that are building great independent and egalitarian nations.

"I never forget that day," an Eritrean cameraman exclaimed, during my visit to his country. I had just finished an assignment inside the Presidential Palace. Then I met my friends and we were having coffee in front of the main gate. Suddenly the Western networks began broadcasting that frantically that 'there is a coup in Asmara'. Social media went bananas. It was the 'Breaking News' story everywhere. And here we were, right there, on a lazy sunny afternoon, in front of the Palace... I had just seen the President.... All was quiet! They just invented it, in order to get people out onto the streets! They were trying to manufacture a coup via their media and social media outlets."

***

It is mainly fear, implanted into the brains of its subjects and slaves; fear that allows the Empire to control almost the entire Planet. Often it is subconscious fear, but it is fear nevertheless. Fear can be that of the Empire as a whole, or of its might and brutality, or even of the alternatives, portrayed in the most unsavory and frightening colors by the propaganda.

In order to rule unopposed, one has to be feared! And one has to smear the alternatives. The task to spread fear, slander diversity and dissent, was given to the official media, academia and 'artists'.

Of course the biggest 'threat' to the Empire has been the two sisters who were born under the same star, from the same mother called Humanism. Their names are Communism and Socialism. And I am not only talking about the Western Marxist concept. Now there are many great concepts that put life and the well being of the people first, all over the world!

In fact, a few decades ago, it was becoming crystal clear that Western colonialism, imperialism and capitalism seemed to be finished. Their time was up! Socialism was the natural and logical way forward for most of humanity.

But then the West and its Empire fought back. They employed extreme violence and brutality, as well as cunning 'divide and rule' tactics. Tens of millions died, and progress was stopped, although hopefully, only for a limited period of time. And not everywhere!

One of many reasons why Russia is perceived as a great 'threat' is because it inherited the humanist and internationalist foreign policy of the Soviet Union. But, also because it itself is actually becoming socialist again (although it is moving in that direction by taking extremely short steps). Russia is recovering irreversibly from those dark days of the free marketer and West's lackey, Boris Yeltsin.

Russia is also hated because it is setting the 'wrong example'; proving to the world that one can develop and prosper without taking orders from the West, without serving its governments and corporations. Or more precisely: it can do it exactly because it broke itself free!

The demonization of Russia is relentless. Every little negative detail is multiplied and magnified by the mainstream media and film industry. The world's public is being nourished by bizarre stereotypes and fabrications. And so one of the most compassionate, deep, artistic and passionate nations on Earth, Russia, is depicted as being cold, robotic, heartless and inherently evil.

Massive NATO military forces are now

dispatched along Russia's western border, and they include German troops (an outrageous fact, considering the history). Periodically there are maneuvers and exercises, not far from the borderline. It is clearly a provocation, and it all brings back the horrific memories of the years right before World War II, the war in which the Russian nation lost between 25 and 30 million lives. A few hundred kilometers south, an old ally, in fact a Slavic sister, Ukraine, is being forced to confront Russia by its Western handlers, something that is being done against the will of the great majority of the Ukrainian people.

The US is heavily involved in the destabilizing of Central Asia, including a group of nations that used to form part of the Soviet Union.

But thanks to Machiavellian Western propaganda, it is actually Russia that is being portrayed as the aggressor and a danger to world peace!

And it is China—of all great nations—which is being depicted as some kind of a ruthless and unpredictable monster that is now ready to swallow the world! In fact China is an extremely predictable country, and any unbiased student of world history would clearly see how peacefully it has been behaving, for centuries!

But to 'prove' that China is not a Communist country, anymore, and at the same time that it is one of the greatest threats to world peace and 'stability' (read: to Western control of the World), is one of the most important tasks given to the Western media, academia and propagandists by the Empire.

And they are actually succeeding! Indoctrination tactics are working flawlessly. The Western public is by now thoroughly brainwashed (at worst) or confused (at best) when it comes to China. In recent years I engaged hundreds of French, Italian, Spanish, German, British and Czech people, mainly intellectuals, in discussions about China, just to receive (with extremely few exceptions) a barrage of standardized, patronizing, mass-produced 'opinions'. It often felt like talking to the people who were forced to live for decades under the Taliban or under the 'spiritual guidance' of some fundamentalist evangelical Protestant sect.

In fact, China is both Communist

(Communism or Socialism, but with distinct Chinese characteristics) as it is breathtakingly successful! Analyzing this marvelous country, together with my China-based colleagues and comrades, I'm coming to the conclusion that Beijing often uses "capitalist means in order to achieve socialist goals" (to borrow a quote from Jeff J. Brown, which is actually the sub-title' of his latest book).

And an enormous, independent, successful Communist or Socialist country – that is absolutely the worst nightmare for the Empire! It is something that has to be stopped, derailed, destroyed, isolated and demonized by all means!

China's Communist success... You would never hear about that on CNN, BBC or Fox TV!

Just as you would never hear that Indonesia, India, Rwanda and any of the other Empire's allies and client nations, are in fact among the most brutal fascist 'failed' states around, and that the genocides in Papua, Kashmir and the Democratic Republic of Congo (DRC) are the bloodiest extermination campaigns anywhere in the world. I have worked in all these countries, intensively, I can testify. As this is being written, the people of Kashmir are being murdered and tortured. Right at this moment! So are the people of Papua, in the hands of Indonesian racists. So are the Congolese men, women and children, slaughtered by the best allies of the West in Africa – Rwanda and Uganda. I'm wondering how many of my readers are actually aware of it?

***

Perhaps I'm obsessed with "exposing lies of the Empire". A second volume will soon follow my 820-page long book. I cannot stop traveling, investigating and amassing the evidence. Because I am shocked, because I am outraged and because there are so few, so desperately few people that are actually still working in the most devastated parts of the world!

Virtually all stereotypes about the world that have been domesticated in the West are wrong, terribly wrong.

The story of the Russian Revolution is told in the most twisted way, and so is the story of the Ukrainian famine and of the gulags. Not everything is wrong, of course, but the facts and numbers are twisted. I will soon resume my work in the Russian Far East, to write intensively on this subject.

The story of China is grotesquely wrong, from the Great March to the present day!

The story of Cambodia's "Commie slaughter" under the Khmer Rouge is a thoroughly idiotic manipulation! The slaughter was there, but more people died from the US carpet-bombing, and then from being displaced from their farms by US mines and cluster 'bombies', than from Pol Pot's atrocities. The great majority of Khmer Rouge men and women had nothing to do with Communism. They were just settling scores with the capitalists, which they saw as responsible for selling the country to the US, and for the bombing of their countryside. In the jungle, I recently met Pol Pot's personal guard. He told me frankly that he was simply pissed off (the bombing killed many of his relatives), and had no clue what Communism was: "Pol Pot came and said 'Communism! Let's fight the traitors!' And we did. How could someone call us a Communist country if we did not even know what Communism was?"

What we hardly ever hear is the most important story of mankind: the story of Western colonial plunders, of imposed slavery, genocides that lasted for centuries, of British-triggered famines that killed tens of millions in the Sub-Continent, of virtually the entire Europe and Christianity systematically committing global holocaust. We are not told that it actually happened, and that it is still going on and on and on!

In order to 'shelter' the Western public from the horrendous truth about the past and the present of their countries and culture, new and newer stories about those "evil others" are continually being invented and circulated.

Perhaps, soon, we will be really told that Mr. Putin is a vampire, or that Kim Jong Un is eating Korean virgins for breakfast. We may not be far from such a new wave of propaganda zeal.

It all makes sense: the more evil the Empire becomes; the more it has to smear its adversaries. Nazi Germany was operating in the same mode.

The mass media and Hollywood are asked to perform and to deliver results.

And they do! Reality and fiction are now being systematically mixed, and everything gets blurred and finally the great confusion and intellectual chaos are managing to overwhelm both reason and logic.

The Empire is killing millions and destroying countries and continents. But California is falling off a cliff, and clouds of huge insects are invading the entire North America. While millions of alien terrorists are now engulfing the 'tolerant' and 'democratic' Europe! So what is more terrible? Plus there are those sinister monsters like Count Vlad and Comrade Kim, waiting with their daggers behind each and every corner!

Therefore, The Empire and its people have to 'protect' themselves. They have to be tough, even tougher than before! And to put their interests first! America (North America) first! Germany first! France first!

Primitive? Does it all sound primitive? Yes, certainly. But it works! At least for the Europeans and North Americans it does. And the rulers don't give a damn what works or doesn't for the rest of the Planet.

August 20, 2016

8
Unreliability, Spinelessness of The Western 'Left'

It is tough to fight any real war. And it takes true guts, discipline and determination to win it.

For years and decades, the so-called 'left' in the West has been moderately critical of North American (and sometimes even of European) imperialism and neo-colonialism. But whenever some individual or country rose up and began openly challenging the Empire, most of the Western left-wing intellectuals simply closed their eyes. They refused to offer their full, unconditional support to those who were putting their lives (and often even the existence of their countries) on the line.

I will never forget all those derogatory punches directed at Hugo Chavez, punches coming from members of the 'anti-Communist left', after he dared to insult George W. Bush at the United Nations in 2006, calling him a "devil" and choking, theatrically, from the sulfur that was still 'hanging in the air' after the US President's appearance at the General Assembly.

I will not be dropping names here, but readers would be surprised if they knew how many of those iconic leaders of the US left wing, described Chavez and his speech as 'impolite', 'counter-productive', and even 'offensive'.

Tens of millions of people have died because of Western imperialism, after WWII. Under the horrid leadership of George W Bush (and later Obama and Clinton) Afghanistan, Libya, Syria and Iraq have been reduced to ruins... But one has to remain 'polite', 'objective' and cool headed?

Well, that is not how real revolutions have been ignited. This is not how the successful anti-colonialist wars are fought. When the real battle begins, 'politeness' is actually mostly unacceptable, simply because the oppressed masses are endlessly pissed off, and they want their feelings to be registered and expressed forcefully by the leaders. Even the search for 'objectivity' is often out of place, when still fragile revolutions have to face the entire monumental hostile propaganda of the regime (of the Empire), as well as foreign sponsored 'opposition', NGOs and corrupt 'civil societies'.

Chavez actually received very little support from Western 'left-wing' intellectuals. And now when Venezuela is bleeding, the 'Bolivarian Republic' can only count on a handful of revolutionary Latin American nations, as well as on China, Iran and Russia; definitely not on some robust, organized and militant solidarity from the left wing in Western countries.

I'd go even further and ask: do most of the Western leftists really support revolutions and anti-colonialist struggles of the oppressed world?

I actually believe that they don't. And this is clearly visible from reading most of the so-called alternative media in both North America and Europe.

Whoever stands up, whoever leads his nation into battle against the Western global dictatorship, is almost immediately defined as a demagogue. He or she is most likely christened 'undemocratic', and not just by the mass and 'liberal' media, but also on the pages of the so-called 'alternative' and 'progressive' Western press. Not all, but some, and frankly: most of it!

Cuba received even less support than Venezuela. After the collapse of the Soviet Union, no attempt was actually made by Western leftists to bail the heroic nation out. It was China, in the end, which ran to its rescue and saved Cuban socialism. (When I wrote about it, I got hundreds of Western leftists at my throat, and in the end it took Fidel himself to confirm, in his 'Reflections', what I was saying, to get them off my back). Then, when the Obama administration began making dangerous advances on Havana, almost everyone in the West began screwing those cynical grimaces: 'you see; now everything will collapse! They will buy Cuba!' Well, they didn't. I travelled to the beloved green island, and it was so clear from the first moments there, that the 'revolution is not for sale'. But you will not read it often in the Western 'progressive' media.

It is of course not just Latin America that is 'disliked' by the 'progressives' in the West. Actually, Latin America is still at least getting some nominal support in London, Paris and New York.

China and Russia, two powerful nations, which are now standing openly against Western imperialism, are despised by virtually all 'liberals' and by most of the Western 'left'. In those circles, there is total ignorance about the Chinese type of democracy, about its ancient culture, and about its complex but extremely successful form of Communism (or call it 'socialism with Chinese characteristics'). Like parrots, the Western leftists repeat the mainstream liberal propaganda that 'China is being capitalist', or that it is being ruled by 'state capitalism'. The internationalism of Chinese foreign policy is constantly played down, even mocked.

Openly racist and ignorant hostility of the Western 'left' towards China has disgusted many Chinese leaders and intellectuals. I only realized the extent of this revulsion, when I spoke, last year, at the First World Cultural Forum in Beijing, and mingled with the thinkers at the China Academy of Social Sciences, the right (intellectual) arm of the government and the Party.

China can count on its allies in Russia, Latin America, Africa and elsewhere, but definitely not in the West.

It is pointless to even mention Russia, Philippines, Syria or South Africa.

The downing of MH17 was followed by more blatant anti-Russian propaganda. The West was prepared to milk this cynical false flag for all the mileage it could. The unkindest cut was the silence or collaborationist stance adopted by many nominal leftists.

Russia, 'the victim' during the horrid Yeltsin years was 'embraced' by the Western left. Russia the warrior, Russia the adversary to Western imperialism, is, once again, loathed.

It appears that the 'progressives' in the United States and Europe really prefer 'victims'. They can, somehow, feel pity and even write a few lines about the 'suffering of defenseless women and children' in the countries that the West is plundering and raping. That does not extend to all countries that are being brutalized, but at least to some...

What they don't like at all, are strong men and women that have decided to fight: to defend their rights, to face the Empire.

The Syrian government is hated. The North Korean government is despised. The President of the Philippines is judged by Western liberal media measures: as a vulgar freak who is killing thousands of 'innocent' drug pushers and consumers (definitely not as a possibly new Southeast Asian Sukarno who is willing to send the entire West to hell).

Whatever the Western 'left' thinks about North Korea and its government (and in fact, I think, it cannot really think much, as it is fully ignorant about it), the main reason why the DPRK is hated so much by the Western regime, is because it, together with Cuba, basically liberated Africa. It fought for the freedom of Angola and Namibia, it flew Egyptian MIGs against Israel, it struggled in Rhodesia (now Zimbabwe) as well as in many other countries, and it sent aid, teachers and doctors to the entire continent devastated by the Western colonialist barbarity.

Much good it received in return! At best, indifference, at worse, total spite!

Some say that the Western 'left' doesn't want to take power, anymore. It lost all of its important battles. It became toothless, impotent, and angry about the world and itself.

When in January 2016 I spoke at the Italian Parliament (ending up insulting the West for its global plunder, hypocrisy), I mingled a lot with the 5 Star Movement, which had actually invited me to Rome. I spent time with its radical left wing. There are some great people there, but overall, it soon became clear that this potentially the biggest political movement in the country is actually horrified of coming to power! It does not really want to govern.

But then, why call those weak bizarre selfish Western entities the 'left wing' parties and movements? Why confuse terms, and by that, why discredit those true revolutionaries, those true fighters, who are risking, sacrificing their lives, right now, all over the world?

Wars are all extremely ugly. I have

covered many of them, and I know... But some of them, those that are fought for the survival of humanity, or for survival of the particular countries, are inevitable. One either fights, or the entire Planet ends up being colonized and oppressed, in shackles.

If one decides to fight, then there has to be discipline and single-mindedness; total determination. Or the battle is lost from the very beginning!

When the freedom and survival of one's motherland is at stake, things get very serious, 'dead-serious'. Battle is not a discussion club. It is not some chatting venue, a cafe for political dilettantes, or a living room couch.

If we, as 'leftists', have already once decided that imperialism and colonialism (or 'neo-colonialism') are the greatest evils destroying our humanity, then we have to show discipline and join ranks, and support those who are at the frontline; if we are not at the frontline ourselves.

Otherwise we will become an irrelevant laughingstock, and history will and should judge us harshly, even mercilessly!

September 30, 2016

Andre Vltchek

9
Western "Culture" is Wrecking Entire Continents

You say "European cultural institutions", and what should come immediately to mind are lavish concerts, avant-garde art exhibitions, high quality language courses and benevolent scholarships for talented cash-strapped local students.

It is all so noble, so civilized!

Or, is it really? Think twice!

I wrote my short novel, *"Aurora"*, after studying the activities of various Western 'cultural institutions', in virtually all the continents of the Planet. I encountered their heads; I interacted with the 'beneficiaries' of various funding schemes, and I managed to get 'behind the scenes'.

What I discovered was shocking: these shiny 'temples of culture' in the middle of so many devastated and miserable cities worldwide (devastated by the Western imperialism and by its closest allies – the shameless local elites), are actually carefully linked to Western intelligence organizations. They are directly involved in the neo-colonialist project, which is implemented virtually on all continents of the world, by North America, Europe, Taiwan, Japan and few other countries.

'Culture' is used to re-educate and to indoctrinate mainly the children of the local elites. Funding and grants are put to work where threats and killing were applied before. How does it work? It is actually all quite simple: rebellious, socially oriented and anti-imperialist local artists, academics and thinkers are now brazenly bought and corrupted. Their egos are played on with great skill. Journeys abroad are easily arranged, funding dispersed, scholarships offered.

Carrots are too tasty, most would say, 'irresistible'. Seals of approval from the Empire are ready to stamp those blank pages of the lives of still young, unrecognized but angry and sharp young artists and intellectuals from those poor, colonized countries. It is so easy to betray! It is so easy to bend.

Some, very few nations are in this sense almost incorruptible, like Cuba. But Cuba is a unique country. *"Patria no se vende!"* they say there, or in translation "One does not sell Fatherland!" But one, unfortunately, does sell it, almost everywhere else in the world: from Indonesia to Turkey, from Kenya to Colombia and India.

***

"Aurora" begins in a small cafe in an ancient city in Indonesia (which is not called Indonesia). Hans, the German head of an unnamed cultural institute is talking to his local 'disciples'. He loves his life here: all the respect he gets, those countless females he is sexually possessing and humiliating, the lavish lifestyle he is allowed to lead.

A woman enters; a beautiful woman, a proud woman, an artist, a woman who was born here but who left, many years ago, for far away Venezuela. Her name is Aurora. Her husband is Orozco, a renowned revolutionary painter. Aurora's sister was killed in this country, because she refused to give up her revolutionary art. She was kidnapped, tortured, raped, and then murdered. Hans, the head of a European cultural organization, was involved.

Aurora confronts Hans, and in reality, the entire European culture of plunder and colonialism.

And that night she is joined, she is supported, by Wolfgang Amadeus Mozart, or more precisely, by his merry ghost, who is thoroughly disgusted of being used as one of the symbols of the 'culture' which destroyed him personally, which destroyed the very essence of the arts, and which has been in fact destroying, for centuries, this entire Planet.

***

When I recently shared the plot of *"Aurora"* with a local 'independent' filmmaker in Khartoum, Sudan, he first listened attentively, and then with horror, and in the end he made a hasty dash towards the door. He escaped, not even trying to hide his distress. Later I was told that he is fully funded by Western 'cultural institutions'.

After reading it, my African comrades, several leading anti-imperialist fighters, immediately endorsed the book, claiming that it addressed some of the essential problems their continent is facing.

The cultural destruction the Empire is spreading is similar everywhere: in Africa, Asia and in Latin America.

I wrote *"Aurora"* as a work of art, as fiction. But I also wrote it as a *J'accuse*, as a detailed study of cultural imperialism.

My dream is that it would be read by millions of young thinkers and artists, on all continents, that it would help them to understand how the Empire operates, and how filthy and disgraceful betrayal could be.

November 4, 2016

Andre Vltchek

10

The Entire World is "Fake News"

Imperialist demagogues, as well as religious fanatics, are known to live in their grotesque realities. They erect huge sand castles, invent mascots, and bombard the public relentlessly with self-promoting messages. Those who refuse to listen and believe, those who dare to doubt and resist, are sidelined, starved to death, humiliated or simply liquidated.

Western religions and European/North American brutal colonialist practices are intertwined culturally. Hand in hand, for centuries, they have been destroying our Planet, from corner to corner, on all continents and even on the high seas.

All conquests, all genocides, all plunders have been eternally rationalized, painstakingly justified. Grand bogus concepts of charity, of 'altruism' have been erected. Subjugated nations have always been ruined in the name of some higher principles, in order to save them from themselves. For centuries, the West has portrayed itself as a sacrificial lamb, as a hand chosen by some divine power, as the greatest civilization that is continuously and altruistically liberating the world.

In the West, scribblers and 'scholars' have been paid to soften every barbarity committed by the rulers, soldiers and even common citizens.

The cults of formal learning, of facts and information have been erected. Holed up in innumerable officially recognized institutions, the scholars, certified demagogues, researchers and media people have been 'studying' each other, recycling and quoting each other, filling millions of books with essentially the same narrative.

'New' and 'revolutionary' academic discoveries mostly lead to the same old conclusions, to stale intellectual and moral passivity, cowardice and spinelessness.

Endless libraries have been filled with useless volumes, first arriving in print, then later in electronic form. Tens of millions of young and not too young men and women are busy wasting their lives, chasing diplomas, those colorful pieces of paper with the seal of approval, certifying people as fit to serve the Empire and the victorious civilization.

At some point, all major philosophical and existential topics ceased to be discussed, in official academia, in mainstream media, in the film houses, libraries and on the pages of best selling books.

No one paid any attention to this trend. The world simply 'moved forward'.

The 'issues' did not disappear. Genocides are still administered by the West in order to plunder the world, the world of the 'un-people'.

Western colonialism was never really stopped or defeated.

Great ideologies based on humanism were successfully smeared, even erased from the sub-consciousness of the people. Gutless masses, but especially cowardly intellectuals, got convinced that it would be the best 'not to take stances', and not to wear 'old labels' and gather under 'old flags'. Passivity combined with the extreme selfishness eventually mutated into collaboration with the regime.

The environment has been getting ruined, progressively and irreversibly.

The press, mass media, gained mastery in saying nothing, addressing nothing, criticizing nothing related to the plunder of the world, and to the suppression of new and truly revolutionary ideas.

Enormous hordes of teachers, lawyers, scientists, and bureaucrats got converted into fundamental idiots, but armed with their licenses, bar exams, patents, contracts and other 'feel-good' sheets of colorful papers.

Tens of millions of lawyers failed to form even one single powerful international organization fighting for justice, against the terror of the Empire.

This make-believe world has by now managed to expel Reality and become 'real' itself in the minds and brains of billions of men, women and children.

True Reality went underground. She had to become a fugitive, a refugee, paperless and disrespected, belonging nowhere.

She is roaming our Planet, searching for

scattered allies, for those few human beings who are still not fully indoctrinated, or fully sold.

Whenever she is caught, she is beaten, stripped naked, and humiliated. A piece of paper saying 'A Lie' is hanged around her neck.

Those who are still standing tall, defending great ideals, fateful to the 'old labels', are being ridiculed. Old flags, under which millions used to march forward, often victoriously, are now being dirtied, defecated on.

Whatever contradicts the Empire is gradually labeled as Fake News.

In the West, no one seems to be noticing. There are no mass demonstrations, no clashes with police, as laws and regulations are being changed and entire Constitutions violated.

It is because an overwhelming majority is actually collaborating with the regime.

It is because it is suddenly so frightening, or at least impractical, to think outside the box.

It is because there are very few examples of intellectual courage left in this world.

Fake News, fake history, fake emotions, and fake ideals... Everything that is not supporting the official narrative is slowly but seemingly irreversibly becoming 'fake'.

The only way forward, and the only way for our humanity to survive, would be for at least one group of extremely bright people to fully break from that straightjacket put on the world by the Empire, to reject official perceptions and 'knowledge', and to completely cast off all major tools of analyses of Christian and Western supremacy ideologies which are still functioning as the main 'intellectual' pillars of the Empire and its collaborators in the colonies.

One's thought, in order to be original and revolutionary, would have to be almost completely cleansed, even isolated, from the official propaganda of the Empire, from its movies and music, from its schools on all levels, from its professionally manipulative narratives.

Diplomas and licenses supplied by the indoctrination institutions should be used as toilet paper for extremely severe cases of intellectual food poisoning, and flushed immediately, together with all that toxic shit that consists of so called 'facts' and 'news'.

***

While the 'Real News' package is being disseminated all over the world by the Imperial propaganda machine, hundreds of millions of 'un-people' are continuing to die annually, aimlessly.

Many are actually vanishing while still fully believing in every word of what they had been fed by the news channels and newspapers. Would they be told the truth (now also known in the West as 'Fake News'), they'd most likely refuse to die, even opting to fight for their survival.

Fight against whom, against the Empire? That would be unacceptable. Therefore, alternative sources of information must be immediately suppressed – exactly what the Nobel Peace Prize laureate President Obama has been aiming at during the last months of this year, before stepping down from his throne.

The Empire is in panic, because resistance in the form of alternative thoughts and concepts is now coming from various parts of the world, especially from those areas not yet infested with the English-language (as well as French or German) standardized storyline. It comes from such places as China's Academy of Social Sciences, from several Russian institutions and many fiction and non-fiction writers, as well as from numerous new and not so new media outlets in Latin America and even Africa and the Middle East.

It is now easy to imagine that the Empire might soon introduce some fascist institution like a "Department of Truth". Its employees could start demanding that each essay and book is 'well researched', insisting on 'facts'.

Writing and philosophy could be reduced to the level of present-day academia: only recycled thoughts would be acceptable. It would not be enough to say that last week it was raining four days a week. A suitable alternative would be: "Last week it was raining four times a week, according to Professor Sigmund Brown." Or even better: "Both Professors Brown and Green agreed that last week it was raining four times a week". Then, footnotes would have to be supplied, as well as other information.

Otherwise – it could be defined as Fake News.

The Fake News clause could be invoked if someone wrote, for instance "the true and the most brutal terrorist in modern history is the West." Or "Several hundreds of millions of people were slaughtered by European empires, and then by the US Empire, in the last several centuries. This holocaust took place in Africa, Asia, what is now known as Latin America, in the Middle East and Oceania, basically everywhere. No alternative system including those of the Soviet Union or China ever came close to the barbarity committed by the West."

Anyone spreading such blasphemy, such sacrilege, could be caught, charged, tried, punished, and 'neutralized'.

Just imagine, someone writing this: "All basic narratives on which Western propaganda is based, are either false, or at least have been heavily twisted and manipulated. This includes all storylines related to the Soviet Union, China, colonialism and the anti-colonialist struggle, Cambodia, Cuba, and even

Rwanda. The list is long. Ignorance of the Western public is almost complete."

How could this not be identified as 'Fake News'? No Professor Blue would utter such judgment, and no Professor Pink would confirm it. You can spend your time digging your snout into millions of books in official libraries, but only handful of them would mention it.

Therefore, it is all fake, all fabricated. It does not exist, and should be forbidden, censored.

You can of course hear all this in Havana, Caracas, Beijing, Moscow or Johannesburg. In Beijing, in a normal big state-run bookstore there is much greater variety of political opinion than on the entire island of Manhattan. Even many common folks in non-Western places know things and pronounce them freely. However, 'unapproved' people cannot be trusted, can they? Especially when it concerns such explosive pieces of material! Also, foreigners speaking their strange twisted tongues cannot be trusted.

Actually, nothing and nobody can be trusted!

Fake News is everywhere, creeping,

ambushing us behind each corner. If the Empire is not vigilant, Western supremacy may one day collapse. Which would be against God's will... Oh, sorry, that was a slip! The correct way to put it: It would be against all reason, against all logic and all facts.

President Obama cares, he understands.

And soon we will be defended with even greater fervor: as now comes Donald Trump!

January 9, 2017

11
"Outside World", According to Western Liberals

Most likely you have already heard that tune, ten times, or maybe one hundred, depending where you live and the circle of friends you have. But let me remind you how it goes: "I'll never set foot in Singapore, because it is all business there." Or: "Let others go to Gulf countries, I'd never do something like that. They have no culture and it is all showing off and glitz there, purchased with oil money... not to mention all those terrible conflicts they are fueling in the region." Then, there is that big ugly "I" name: "Me going there? Over my dead body! It is illegitimate; it is sitting on other peoples' land."

So it goes...

While genuine criticism is always healthy, it is important to realize that many of those who get ignited by even hearing the names of places like Dubai or Singapore are actually living in the cities like New York, Paris or London. Some are even practicing law, or other mainstream professions that have to be defined as the true mainstays of Western regimes.

Most of those opinionated individuals regurgitating a variety of clichés are actually extremely selective in choosing the targets of their rage. They like playing it safe. Some admit that they are actually cowards, and would never openly rock the boat, never identify with any 'radical' (according to them, even being 'Marxist' or 'revolutionary' is 'radical' or 'extreme') labels, as they'd never march publicly under any (especially if the color is red) flag.

We are talking about 'progressive liberals', or 'moderate leftists' or 'those who sympathize with the left, but go by particular issues': well, liberals in short.

Some are Westerners, locally 'produced' (or should we say 'mass-produced'), but others actually live in the West but even come from countries such as Iraq, Afghanistan or Libya, places thoroughly shattered by Western imperialism.

Only a few of my friends (and I respect those few very much for their proud and decisive stand) would ever say: "I'll never go to London, because Brits murdered directly or indirectly few hundred millions of human beings, and in a way they are doing it until now."

If you boycott Dubai or Singapore, shouldn't New York or London actually be on the top of your list? Unless you actually live there, enjoying countless benefits financed by imperialist plunder. And if you are not so 'pure' yourself, then don't be too fussy about others, and about the 'secondary centers of evil'.

"There is nothing more pathetic than 'moderate movements' and individuals, than 'moderately progressive masses'. They kill the very essence of human existence, which is, of course, rebellion. No progress could ever come from intellectual or political moderation. Genius is always extreme. Courage is extreme!

There is plenty of shouting originating

from millions of comfy couches in the living rooms of the US, UK, France or Germany, but too little appetite or *cojones* to organize, show discipline and hard work, or to join some good old-fashioned revolution or a revolutionary movement, the only actions that could still actually make some real change in those depressing, paralyzed societies that are always living at someone else's expense, from someone else's sweat and blood, while continuously reserving 'rights' to moralize and to pass lofty judgments against others.

While mainstream 'left-leaning liberals' are constantly ridiculing Western pop and the mainstream (including, of course, Western media), most of their references actually come from exactly those sources! Take them to Asia, Latin America or Africa, and their ignorance would shine like that famous Cape of Good Hope lighthouse.

Outside of the realm of West-centered stereotypes, they know very little, or close to nothing, but they have always 'their own' opinion, about everything and about every place.

Their assessments of places like

Ecuador, Philippines, China, Russia or Syria are based on thoroughly mainstream logic. Or sorry, they are actually based on the 'liberal' or 'moderately progressively' mainstream logic.

If a traditional Latin American or Asian revolutionary were to be locked, as a cruel punishment, with such person or group of people in the same room for two or three months, he or she would go insane, in the end perhaps murdering them, or committing suicide. Soft Western (or Westernized) left/mainstream left-leaning liberals and people of true revolutionary left are two opposites with absolute zero tolerance for each other (but plenty of genuine allergy).

Once I spent a long evening in a pub in Manila with my Chinese revolutionary Marxist friend, a musician, and a British human rights lawyer. The encounter was truly Kafkaesque. Although they debated in English (my friend's English was perfect), it often appeared that they both needed an interpreter.

I recently watched with great delight a television debate (in fact a duel) between my Argentinian friend and comrade, left-wing historian Néstor Gorojovsky, and some Spanish 'progressive' self appointed 'judge' of the Presidents Assad and Putin. Their relatively polite exchange lasted for approximately 2 minutes. What followed were naked insults. It was truly delightful to watch! It just so rarely happens in the West and especially when English language is used, that such great thinker like Néstor would explode live on TV and suddenly employ fitting gutter language (the only one that he actually really wants to use on such an occasion) attacking and defining his archenemy – a 'moderate', mainstream, cowardly and submissive leftist. Of course the language that was used on the program was Spanish.

Oh, how scared are liberals of such explosions! How much they hate it when first Chavez and then Duterte unleashed it in front of television cameras, even at the United Nations! Their hate is simply because they'd never dare to confront the establishment, the global regime, at least not publicly, not outside their pub. It is 'too impolite', 'too vulgar', isn't it? Or is it actually just too impractical?

In London and New York, they dance

like animals, like maniacs, drunk or stoned in their clubs, wagging buttocks to the most absurd and primitive rhythms, but to shout insults at the mass murderers is 'vulgar'.

Yes, there is nothing more pathetic than 'moderate movements' and individuals, than 'moderately progressive masses'. They kill the very essence of human existence, which is, of course, rebellion. No progress could ever come from intellectual or political moderation. Genius is always extreme. Courage is extreme! Only a coward could call for upholding the law or for some static, boring, despotic harmony (like that promoted by Confucius or now by Western liberalism).

In 1911, the great Czech novelist Jaroslav Hašek, launched his political party – Strana mírného pokroku v mezích zákona. Loosely translated into English it means "Party of Measured Progress, Within the Parameters of Law". It was a joke, of course, a typical Czech intellectual piss take. Hašek knew perfectly well, that no progress could be 'measured', and no true change could ever be 'legal'.

***

The problem is that Western mainstream liberals, and even their lawyers (¡Ay, qué horror!) actually do travel abroad. Many go far away, as far as Asia, Latin America, even Africa. And they bring with them their little, scared, conformist, indecisive and essentially cowardly world.

Their guilt from overindulging and doing nothing and challenging nothing at home, converts into a species of violently distasteful political correctness. Abroad they feel like 'overcompensating'. They become excessively polite to hotel and airline staff, to porters and waitresses. Some even begin making their own beds in five-star hotels. They are constantly looking for 'real people', for 'traditional places' and for 'real life'. It is pointless to show or to explain anything to them: they trust exclusively and arrogantly, their 'own instinct' only, which was (of course they'd passionately deny it), formed by the mainstream media back in the US, UK, France, or elsewhere in the West.

Tell them the truth that a 'real' Thai or Vietnamese family would rather eat out in a Japanese or Korean restaurant than in traditional local eatery, and they'd spit in your face. You would trigger the same reaction, if you tried to deconstruct their preconceptions about Zimbabwe, Soviet Union, Syria, or present day Philippines.

Intellectually, their 'good intentions' often do more harm than Western spy agencies. The best would be to prevent them (somehow) from interacting with local intelligentsias (to avert contamination), as all they bring with them are boorish clichés, passivity, spinelessness, and yes, embarrassing ignorance!

In a way (but don't tell them, please), they are like Obama or the Clintons. They know how to talk, but there is no substance, no true passion, no poetry, and no fire behind their perfect pronunciation. Their gutlessness morally corrupts.

They have no ideology, and no beliefs. Their passions are shallow and short-lived. Their world is surreal. It kills; their world murders all higher aspirations, it chokes dreams, it gags revolutionary shouts and blocks any courageous action!

***

The World according to the Western liberals is an extremely orderly place. Paradoxically, most of them 'don't trust any government', and some even call themselves 'anarchists' (my goodness, I cannot imagine any of them breaking even the speed limit, let alone a window! What anarchy, bordello!?).

If you leave it up to them, nothing would ever change. When Fidel died, many of them were 'heartbroken', but the closest they ever got to him was Hotel Tropicana in Havana, or that tourist trap La Bodeguita de Medio. As steamy Buena Vista Social Club (brought to the limelight in the West by a German film director Wim Wenders) is their symbol of Cuban music, Fidel and Che personify their secret 'dark' dreams, periodically reminding them what they lost or betrayed, what is truly human, and what they will never manage to become, anymore!

They admire science, partially because they absolutely don't understand it, but mainly because it symbolizes some sort of opposite to the most beautiful and most powerful human instincts (which they lost many years ago): passionate and irrational belief in much better world, an unconditional and single-minded loyalty to the cause (exactly what made both Fidel and Che defeat oppressive and reactionary forces), as well as emotions and instincts that are always much more precious and human than any logic or reason!

***

If you'd get locked in the same room with 'them', you'll soon lose all your ability to create, to think imaginatively, and to struggle. If you were in the middle of writing a novel, you'd lose your plot. If you were charging, metaphorically running towards the enemy lines, you'd stumble and fall.

If you'd spend too much time in that room, you would betray. Even longer, and you'd die, at least as an independent, free thinker, and a dreamer. Your flags and your beloved labels would be dragged through dirt. Your essence would be questioned and challenged. Nothing would remain pure, nothing sacred.

The world of the Western (or Westernized) mainstream liberals is like a swamp. You should never come close to it. There is no need to be close. There is nothing there for you. One wrong step and you will die, for nothing, for absolutely nothing. Of course that 'nothing' is nor really 'nothing'; it consists of passivity, of lazy cowardice (intellectual, artistic, simply human), and it could even be, to some extent, and in a perverse way, attractive. You'd be sucked in, then reshaped and reconditioned, and finally end up like the others, sharing a bed with oblivion.

Most of the world has been already sucked into this, conditioned, lobotomized and 'pacified'.

You know it. You sense it. You saw others being destroyed. Still you and those like you, periodically make those fatal errors and follow the honey-coated voices of the 'moderately-left-leaning-liberal' mermaids, then ending up in a gutter, stripped of all your powers, self-respect and courage.

Three of the most beautiful Russian names, three symbols of existence, are exactly what that swamp is not: Love, Belief and Hope. Add to them Courage, add Loyalty, and you get Life. The essence of it is what you get. Something great and worth living and fighting for, something that has been, temporarily, wiped out from the surface of Earth, by 'reason' which is not real reason at all, by illogical logic, by kitschy and cheap feelings, by unsavory surrogates of love, by inability to trust, to believe, and to stand tall and proud, against all odds, against the entire world, if that is what the moment is calling for.

Only with Love, Belief and Hope, big battles for the benefit of humanity can be won. If all three were present, then two beautiful sisters – Courage and Loyalty – would definitely come and stay. Rationality and logic can make life more comfortable, sometimes, but only if there actually still is some life left.

The "outside world" is in turmoil, once again. Rebellion against the Western regime, against the Empire is brewing. These are good days; this is the era that will be remembered by future generations.

Let us keep Western mainstream liberals at bay. Let's not allow their nihilism, their neurotic selfishness, ignorance, emotional laziness and passivity influence that great reawakening that is taking place on all continents of the world.

Let them remain on their couches and in their pubs.

And let us get to work: first constructing the barricades under our beloved and now undusted labels and flags, and then (after the victory) rebuilding the world!

February 3, 2017

12
The West is Finished, But Why?

Despite certain economic and social setbacks, the Western Empire is doing remarkably well. That is, if we measure success by the ability to control the world, to condition the brains of human beings on all continents, and to crush almost all substantial dissent, at home and abroad.

What has almost entirely disappeared from life, at least in such places as New York, London or Paris, is that simple human joy, which is so obvious and evident when it exists. Paradoxically, in the very centers of power, most people seem to be living anxious, unfulfilled, almost frightened lives.

It all somehow doesn't feel right. Shouldn't citizens of the conquering part of the world, of the victorious regime, be at least confident and optimistic?

Of course there are many reasons why they are not, and some of my comrades have already outlined in detail and in colorful language at least the main causes of depression and dissatisfaction with life, which are literally devouring alive those hundreds of millions of European and North American citizens.

The situation is mostly analyzed from a socioeconomic angle. However, I think that the most important causes for the present state of things are much simpler: the West and its colonies almost entirely destroyed the most essential human instincts: people's ability to dream, to feel passionate about things, to rebel and to 'get involved'.

Single-mindedness, optimism, naiveté are almost entirely gone. But those are exactly the qualities that used to move our human race forward!

Despite what is now commonly perceived in the West, it is not 'knowledge' and definitely not 'science' that were behind the greatest leaps forward achieved by civilization.

It has always been a deep and

instinctive humanism, accompanied by faith (and here I'm not talking about some religious faith) and by tremendous dedication and loyalty to the cause. Without naïveté, without innocence, nothing great could have ever been attained.

Science was always there, and it was important for improving many practical aspects of human life, but it was never the main engine propelling a nation towards some just, balanced, and 'livable' society. When employed by an enlightened system, science has played an important role in building a much better world, but it was never the other way around.

Progress was always triggered and fueled by human emotions, by seemingly irrational and unachievable dreams, by poetry and wide scale burning of passions. The finest concepts for improvement of civilization were frequently not even logical; they were simply born out of some beautiful human instincts, intuitions and desires (logic was applied later, when practical details had to be nailed down).

Now 'knowledge', rationality and 'logic', at least in the West, are forcing human feelings into a corner. 'Logic' is now even replacing traditional religions. Obsession with 'facts', with 'understanding' everything, is actually becoming absurdly extreme, dogmatic, even fundamentalist.

Constant debates, analyses, and 'looking at things from different angles', leads to nothing but passivity. But taking action is too scary, and people are not used to making dramatic decisions, anymore, or even gestures.

All this fanatical fact collecting often feels unreal, 'metallic', cold and to many of those who are coming from 'the outside' (geographically or intellectually), extremely unnatural.

Let's not forget that 'facts' consumed by the masses and even by the relatively educated Westerners, are generally coming from identical sources. The same type of logic is being used, and several undistinguishable tools of analyses applied. Consuming excessive amount of news, 'facts' and 'analyses' usually doesn't lead to understanding anything in depth, or to truly critical thoughts, quite the contrary – it very effectively murders one's ability to consider totally new concepts, and especially to rebel against the intellectual clichés and stereotypes. No wonder that the European and North American middle classes are among the most conformist people on earth!

Collecting mountains of data and 'information' in most cases leads absolutely nowhere. For millions, it is becoming just a hobby, like any other one, including videogames and PlayStation. It keeps a person 'on top of things', so he or she can impress acquaintances, or it simply satisfies that neurotic need to constantly consume news.

To make things worse, most Westerners are incessantly locked in a complex 'information' and perceptions web with their families, friends and co-workers. There is constant pressure to conform while extremely little space and almost no rewards for true intellectual courage or originality.

Regimes have managed to a great extent to standardize 'knowledge', mainly by utilizing pop culture and indoctrinating people through its 'educational' institutions.

People are actually voluntarily locking

themselves for years in schools and universities, wasting their time, paying their own money, even getting into debt, just in order to make it easier for the regime to indoctrinate them and turn them into good and obedient subjects of the Empire!

Already for decades the system has been successfully producing entire generations of emotionally dead and confused individuals.

These people are so damaged that they cannot fight for anything, anymore (except, sometimes, for their own personal and selfish interests); they cannot take sides, and cannot even identify their own goals and desires. They constantly try (and fail) to 'find something meaningful' and 'fulfilling' they could do in life. It is always about them finding something, not about joining meaningful struggles or inventing something thoroughly new for the sake of humanity! They keep going 'back to school', they keep crying for 'lost opportunities' because they 'didn't study what they think they really should have' (no matter what they actually study or do in life, they mostly feel dissatisfied, anyway).

They are constantly scared of being rejected, they are petrified that their ignorance and inability to do anything truly meaningful would be discovered and ridiculed (many of them actually sense how empty their lives are).

They are unhappy, some thoroughly miserable, and even suicidal. Yet their desperation does not propel them into action. Most of them never rebel; never truly confront the regime, never challenge their immediate milieu.

These hundreds of millions of broken and idle people (some of them actually not stupid at all) are a tremendous loss to the world. Instead of erecting barricades, writing outraged novels or openly ridiculing this entire Western charade, they are mostly suffering in silence.

If the opportunity to thoroughly change their lives really arrives, they cannot identify it, anymore; cannot grasp it. It is because they cannot fight; they were 'pacified' since an early age, since school.

That is exactly where the regime wants to have its citizens. It's where it got them!

Shockingly, almost no one calls this entire nightmare by its real name – a monstrous crime!

People buy books in order to make sense of it all, but they hardly manage to read them to the end. They are too preoccupied; they are lacking concentration and determination. And a great majority of books available in the stores are giving no meaningful answers, anyway.

Still, many are trying: they are analyzing and analyzing, aimlessly. They 'don't understand and want to know'. They don't realize that this path of constantly thinking, while applying certain prescribed tools of the analyses, is one huge trap.

There is really nothing much to understand. People were actually robbed of life, robbed of natural human feelings, of warmth, of passion, even of love itself (what they call 'love' is often a surrogate, and nothing more).

All this is never pronounced not even in fiction books anymore, unless you read in Russian or Spanish. The success of the Empire to produce obedient, scared and unimaginative beings is now complete!

Big corporations are thriving; elites are collecting enormous booty, while a great majority of people in the West are gradually losing their ability to dream and to feel. Without those preconditions, no rebellion is possible. Lack of imagination, accompanied by emotional numbness, is the most effective formula for stagnation, even regression.

This is why the West is finished.

***

The grotesque obsession with science, with medical practices, and with 'facts', is helping to divert attention from real and horrific issues.

Constant debates, analyses, and 'looking at things from different angles', leads to nothing but passivity. But taking action is too scary, and people are not used to making dramatic decisions, anymore, or even gestures.

This also leads to the fact that almost no one in the West is now ready to gather under any ideological banner, or to embrace full heartedly what is called derogatorily 'labels'.

For millennia, people flocked intuitively into various movements, political parties and groups. No significant change was ever achieved by one single individual (although a strong leader at the head of a movement, party or even government could definitely achieve a lot).

To be part of something important and revolutionary was symbolizing often a true meaning of life. People were (and in many parts of the world still are) fully committed, dedicated to important and heroic struggles. Trying to build a better world, fighting for a better world, even dying for it: that was often considered the most glorious thing that a human being could achieve in his or her lifetime.

In the West, such an approach is dead, thoroughly destroyed. There, cynicism reigns. You have to challenge everything, trust nothing, and commit to nothing.

You are expected to mistrust any government. You should ridicule everyone who believes in something, especially if that something is pure and noble. You simply have to drag through filth any grandiose attempt to improve the world, whether it is happening in Ecuador, Philippines, China, Russia or South Africa.

To show strong feeling for some leader,

for a political party or government in a country that is still capable of some fire and passion, is met with mocking sarcasm in places like London or New York. "We are all thieves, and all human beings and therefore governments, are similar", goes the deadly and toxic 'wisdom'.

How lovely, really! What a way forward.

Yes, of course: if hours and hours are spent analyzing some fiery leader or movement, for instance in Latin America, at least some 'dirt' would always emerge, as no place and no group of people are perfect. This gives Westerners a great alibi for not getting involved in anything. That's how it is designed. 'Give up on the hope for a perfect world, say that you simply cannot believe in anything anymore'. Then, go back to school or get yourself some meaningless job.

It is actually much easier than to work extremely hard to save the world or your country! It is much easier than to risk your life and to fight for justice. It is easier than trying to really think, to attempt to invent something thoroughly new, for this beloved and scarred planet of ours!

***

An old Russian ballad says: "It is so hard to love… But it is so easy to leave…"

And with the revolution, with the movements, struggles, even governments that one full heartedly supports, it is, to a great extent, very similar to love.

Love can never be fully scrutinized, fully analyzed, or it is not really love. There is nothing, and should be nothing logical or rational about it. Only when it is dying one begins analyzing, while looking for excuses to slam the door.

But while it is there, while it exists, alive, warm and pulsating, to apply 'objectivity' regarding the other person would be brutal, disrespectful; in a way it would be a betrayal.

Only "new Westerners" can commit such travesty, by analyzing love, by writing 'guides' about how to deal with human feelings, how to maximize profits from their emotional investments!

How could a man who loves a woman just sit on a sofa and analyze: "I love her but maybe I should think twice, because her nose is too big, and her behind is too large?" That's absolute nonsense! A woman who is loved, truly loved, is the most beautiful being on earth.

And so is the struggle!

Otherwise, without true dedication and single-mindedness, nothing will ever change; never improve.

But let's not forget – the Empire doesn't want anything to improve. That's why it is spreading limitless cynicism and nihilism. That's why it is smearing everything pure and natural, while implanting bizarre 'perfection models', so the people always compare, always judge, always have doubts, never feel satisfied, and as a result, abstain from all serious involvements.

The empire wants people to think, but think in a way it programs them to do. It wants them to analyze, but only by using its methods. And it wants people to discard, even reject their natural instincts and emotions.

The results are clear: grotesque individualism and self-centrism, confused, broken societies, collapsed relationships between people, and total spite for higher aspirations.

It is not only about the Marxist or

Andre Vltchek

revolutionary political parties, about the rebellions or internationalist, anti-imperialist struggles.

Have you noticed how shallow, how unstable most inter-human relationships in the West have become? Nobody wants to get truly 'involved'. People are testing each other. They constantly think, hardly feel. Powerful passions are looked down on (emotional outbursts are considered 'indecent', even shameful): now it is suddenly all about one's 'feeling good', always 'calm', but paradoxically, almost no one is actually feeling good or calm in this "new West", anymore.

It all, of course, mutated into the exact opposite of what love, or a true revolutionary work (political, or artistic) used to be, and just to remind you, it used to be the most beautiful, the most insane turmoil, a total departure from dismal normalcy.

In the West, almost no one could even write great poetry, anymore. No haunting melodies, no powerful lyrics are created there.

Life has become suddenly shallow, predictable and programmed.

Without the ability to love passionately, without the capacity to give, to sacrifice everything unconditionally, one cannot expect to become a great revolutionary.

Of course in the passionless West, obsessed with a type of knowledge that somehow keeps failing to enlighten, with the applied sciences and deeply rooted egocentricity, there is no fertile ground for powerful passions left, and therefore no chance for true revolution.

"I rebel: therefore we exist", declared Albert Camus, correctly.

Collective rebellion culminates into revolution. Without a revolution, or without constant aspiration for it, there is no life.

The West has lost the ability to love and to rebel.

And that is why it is finished!

***

There is a good saying: "You can never understand Russia with your brain. You can only believe in it". The same goes for China, Japan and so many other places.

To come to Asia or Russia and begin the

journey by trying to 'understand' these places is nothing short of insanity. There is no reason for it, and no chance that it could be achieved in a few months, even years.

The neurotic and thoroughly Western approach of constantly trying to 'understand' everything with one's brain, can actually ruin all irreversibly and right from the beginning. The best way to start to truly comprehend Asia is by absorbing, by being gently guided by others, by seeing, feeling, discarding all preconceptions and clichés. Understanding doesn't come necessarily with logic. Actually, it almost never does. It involves senses and emotions, and it usually arrives suddenly, unexpectedly.

The revolution, in fact the most sacred and honorable struggles – they also brew for a long time, and they also come unexpectedly, and straight from the heart.

Whenever I come to New York but especially to London or Paris, and whenever I encounter those 'theoretical leftists', I have to smile bitterly when I follow their pointless but long discussions about some theory, which is totally separated from reality. And it is almost exclusively about them: are they Trotskyists and why? Or perhaps they are anarcho-syndicalists? Or Maoists? Whatever they are, they always begin on the couch or a bar stool, and that's where they end up, late in the evening.

In case you are just coming from Venezuela or Bolivia, where people are fighting true battles for the survival of their revolutions, it is quite a shocking experience! Most of them, in Altiplano, have never even heard about Lev Trotsky, or anarcho-syndicalism. What they know is that they are at war, they are fighting for all of us, for a much better world, and they need immediate and concrete support for their struggle: petitions, demonstrations, money, and cadres. All they get is words. They get nothing from the West: almost nothing at all, and they never will.

It is because they are not good enough for the Brits and French. They are too 'real', not 'pure enough'. They make mistakes. They are too human, not sterile, and not 'well-behaved'. They 'violate some rights here or there'. They are too emotional. They are this or that, but definitely 'one could not fully throw his or her weight fully behind them'.

'Scientifically', they are wrong. If one spends ten hours in the pub or living room, discussing them, there would definitely arise enough arguments for withdrawing all support. The same applies for the revolutionaries and for the revolutionary changes in the Philippines, and in so many other places.

The West cannot connect to this way of thinking. It doesn't see absurdity in its own behavior and attitudes. It lost its spirit; it lost its heart, its feelings, from the right and now even from the left. In exchange for what, brain? But there is nothing significant that comes from that area either!

And that is why it is finished!

People are now unwilling to get themselves behind anything real; behind any true revolution, any movement, any government, unless they are like those plastic and toxic looking women from glossy fashion magazines: perfect for men who lost all their imagination and individuality, but thoroughly boring and mass-produced for the rest of us.

February 11, 2017

13

The West Is Becoming Irrelevant, The World Is Laughing

I was recently told by an Asian friend of mine who is working in Paris: "Lately I stopped following almost all that is happening politically in the United States, in the UK and even here in France. It all feels suddenly so irrelevant, a waste of time."

Statements like this would be unimaginable only one decade ago. In the past, what came from Washington and (to a smaller extent) from London was monitored with great attentiveness and fear, all over the world.

But all of a sudden, things have begun to change, rapidly. Despite the extremely

179

violent nature of the Western-designed-and-manufactured global regime, which has been over-imposed on so many parts of the world for decades and centuries, increasing amounts of people in Asia, Latin America and Africa stopped worrying and went leisurely to the 'barricades', beginning to rebel against the perverseness of the 'world order'.

Did it all really happen 'all of a sudden'?

Or were there various catalysts at work, for already quite a substantial period of time?

It is a well-known fact that any deep-seated, chronic anxiety cannot disappear in just a short moment. People who are enslaved, humiliated, scared into obedience, people who are forced to feel uncertain and constantly frightened, cannot reverse their state of mind without some important external factor or set of factors.

It became obvious to me, as I have been working continuously on all continents and in almost all conflict zones of our Planet, that the renewed pride and courage which is now inspiring millions of oppressed human beings, actually came from the decisive and determined stand of just several brave and determined nations, big and small.

The myth about the omnipotence of the Empire has received a few significant blows.

The fable of invincibility has not completely disappeared yet, but at least it has got fractured and gravely injured.

The gate of the terrible prison began cracking. It has not collapsed, but the fractures were wide enough for at least some sunlight to enter the dark and dreadful cavities inhabited by billions of unfortunate and shattered beings.

Some victims stood up immediately; not many but at least some did. Others raised their heads in feeble hope, still lying down on the dirty ground, still chained, and still shaking. That weak light alone entering the dungeon was actually much brighter than what most people ever experienced in their entire life. It has been strong enough to provoke wonderful, brilliant sparks of hope.

***

Except for some temporary setbacks (like in Brazil and Argentina), the anti-imperialist coalition is now steadier than ever; it is determined and constantly expanding.

And it is clearly winning!

It is truly a 'rainbow coalition' of countries, big and small, 'red' and 'pink', even 'green'.

The only unifying factor is the shared determination not to be controlled by Western imperialism and neo-colonialism.

For decades, Cuba stood against the Empire, even after the Soviet block was broken to bits, even when all mutual agreements ceased to be honored by the criminal Yeltsin administration. The Cuban people never surrendered. It is because most of them always believed, from the bottom of their hearts, in socialism and internationalism. And also because they have been convinced that the Western Empire is a morally corrupt and illegitimate entity and therefore has to be resisted.

A small and relatively poor country – Cuba – demonstrated to the entire world that while the Empire is mighty, sadistic and brutal, it is not omnipotent, and it is possible to defy it. There is no reason why one should not dare, or one should not dream about a much better world, why one shouldn't fight for true freedom, attempting to win.

Cuba inspired the world. Its daring Revolution took place just a few miles from the shores of the United States. Soon after, its teachers and doctors went to all parts of the earth, spreading optimism, solidarity and kindness. Its heroic revolutionaries went to fight against the most dreadful forms of colonialism, which were torturing people, is such places as Congo, Angola and Namibia.

After Obama's attempts to water down the determination of the Cuban citizens, many enemies began to predict, cynically:

"Now Cuba will compromise and sell its Revolution."

It never did! I traveled to the Island last year, driving through the countryside, and speaking to people in Havana, Guantanamo and Santiago de Cuba. Almost no one was ready to compromise. A greatly educated nation, Cuba saw through the Empire's tricks and deceptions.

Now almost nobody speaks about the "Cuban compromise", anymore, simply because there isn't any on the table.

China, one of the oldest and greatest civilizations on Earth, went through the terrible period of 'humiliation'. Divided, occupied and plundered by the West, it has never forgotten nor forgiven.

Now the Chinese Communist state and its mixed economy are helping countries in virtually all parts of the world, from Oceania and Latin America, to the Middle East and especially Africa, to survive and to finally stand on their own feet. Despite all the vitriolic propaganda regurgitated by the West (those people in Europe or North America who know close to zero about Africa or China, habitually passing 'confident' and highly cynical 'judgments' about China's involvement in the poor world; judgments based exclusively on the lies and fabrications produced by the Western media), China has been gaining great respect and trust in virtually all corners of the globe.

The Chinese people and their government are now standing firmly against Western imperialism. They will not allow any recurrence of the disgraceful and dreary past.

The West is provoking this mighty and optimistic nation, pushing it into a terrible confrontation. China doesn't want any military conflict. It is the most peaceful, the most non-confrontational large nation on Earth. But it is becoming clear that if pushed against the wall, this time it will not compromise: it will fight.

In the last years I have spoken to many Chinese people, as I traveled to all corners of the country, and I'm convinced that by now the nation is ready to meet strength with strength.

Such determination gives hope to many other countries on our Planet. The message is clear: the West cannot do whatever it wants, anymore. If it tries, it will be stopped. By reason or by force!

Russia is ready again, too. It is standing next to China, enormous and indignant.

Go to Novosibirsk or Tomsk, to Khabarovsk, Vladivostok or Petropavlovsk in Kamchatka. Talk to Russian people and you will soon understand: almost nobody there believes or respects the West, anymore. Throughout history, Russia was attacked and ransacked from the West. Millions, tens of millions of its people were murdered, literally exterminated. And now, the nation is facing what some consider to be yet another imminent attack.

Like the Chinese people, Russians are unwilling to compromise, anymore. The old Russian forecast is once again alive, that very one professed by Alexander Nevsky:

Go tell all in foreign lands that Russia lives! Those who come to us in peace will be welcome as a guest. But those who come to us sword in hand will die by the sword! On that Russia stands and forever will we stand!

In Russia, as in China, and as in so many other nations that were devastated by the Western plunderers, nothing is forgotten and no one is forgotten. It only appeared for a while that the memory had fainted. It never does. You cannot burn down an entire land, ruin the cities, burn the fields, and still pose as one with the moral mandate. Or as we say in Chile: "Justice takes time, but it always comes!"

And the world is watching. It is suddenly clearly registering this determined and brave, epic stand of morally strong nations.

Many of those who are watching are deeply impressed with what they are seeing. Perhaps not in London or in Paris, but go and ask those in Johannesburg or Beirut, or even in Calcutta, Cairo or Buenos Aires. Perhaps you suspect what answers you'd receive there!

Throughout modern history, not once has Iran invaded a foreign country. Yet its secular, progressive and democratic government (under the leadership of Mohammad Mosaddegh) was overthrown in 1953, in a CIA-backed coup. What followed was the monstrosity of the 'pro-Western Shah', and then a horrendous war, an invasion by Iraq, which was also fully backed by the West and which took hundreds of thousands of human lives. Since then, Iran has been suffering from targeted killings of its scientists (by the West and Israel), as well as terrorist attacks also backed from abroad.

Instead of falling on its knees and begging for mercy, Iran defied the West. On several occasions and when provoked, it sent its battleships to the neutral waters near the US coast, and it pledged to defend its land, in case it was to be attacked.

Iran also showed great solidarity towards Latin America, working closely with virtually all of the revolutionary governments there. It stood firmly by Venezuela in a time of great crises, building social housing in Caracas and supporting the *Process* by all other means.

In Latin America, no one will ever forget how former Iranian President Mahmoud Ahmadinejad came to Caracas to attend the funeral of Venezuelan leader Hugo Chavez, his dear friend. During the memorial, the aged mother of Chavez suddenly approached Ahmadinejad, in tears. Breaking all religious protocol of a Shi'a country that he was representing, the Iranian President embraced her, and held her against his heart, until she calmed down.

This moment was expressing one simple and powerful reality: all of us, the internationalists and anti-imperialists, are fighting for the survival of humanity and this planet. There is more that unites us than what is tearing us apart. Once we win, and we will win, the world will be able to find a common language. The West wants to divide us, by spreading hostilities and distrust, all through 'false news' and fabrications. But we understand its game. We will not break our ranks, anymore.

The West is clearly losing. It knows it. It is in panic.

Its nihilism, its propaganda and indoctrination tactics will soon be defeated.

I wrote a lot about the DPRK and how it joined the list of the 'most hated nations on Earth'. It is a well known fact that North Korea was, for years and decades, much richer and more democratic than South Korea (ROK). But it embarked on one tremendous humanist 'project', and together with Cuba, the Soviet Union and to some extent China, it liberated almost the entire African continent, at great cost and sacrifice. And not only that: it sent its top educators and doctors to all corners of the most devastated continent on Earth. Its pilots also flew Egyptian MIGs against Israel, during the 1967 war. These facts have been silenced by Western propaganda, but they clearly explain why the DPRK has been ostracized, pushed to the corner, hit by senseless embargos, and forced to react the way it has been reacting for at least the last two decades.

Andre Vltchek

North Korea has never surrendered either, and it never will.

Neither has Venezuela, for many years the great sentinel and engine of the Bolivarian Revolution, as well as of Latin Internationalism and solidarity. Surviving coups, embargos, plots and propaganda campaigns, surviving attacks, even terror, of the foreign-backed 'opposition', Venezuela has been injured but it is alive. Just a few days ago I spoke to an Italian Parliamentary delegation, consisting of the"5-Star-Movement" MPs, which recently returned from Caracas. Their conclusion was simple: "The worst is over".

The world knows it! Venezuela, DPRK, Cuba – they never fell. No matter how many knives penetrated their bodies, despite so much pain caused by the sanctions, coup attempts and direct acts of terrorism administered by the West and its monstrous Empire.

It is becoming clear and obvious: the West is helpless against determination, true courage and patriotic love. It is powerless when confronted with humanist ideologies, and with true loyalty!

And the world keeps watching, drawing

its conclusions.

I wrote about Syria, comparing Aleppo to the 20th Century Stalingrad. This is where racism, terrorism, and the lowest forms of Western imperialism (and shameful acts of the regional lackeys) were decisively stopped. The price was terrible, but the message to the world extremely clear: The people who love their country with their entire hearts can fight and win against all odds, especially if by their side stand truly great and reliable friends and comrades!

One day the world will thank the Syrian people, profusely and properly. One day, everything will be understood. One day, perhaps soon.

***

This is one of the greatest moments in human history, perhaps the greatest.

It has arrived without big salvos announcing monumental revolutions.

Everything is happening fast, in an organized and determined manner.

The greatest minds of Russia, China, Latin America and the rest of the world, are feverishly, day and night, trying to determine what really brought our world, our civilization, to this ludicrous downfall.

The simplified and stripped-down answer is this: Western imperialism (military, economic and 'intellectual'/'cultural'), colonialism and neo-colonialism, as well as that dreadful by-product of all the above combined –a set of unchecked and savage form of capitalism.

Simultaneously, new forms of government, of economy and social systems are being, once again, planned.

The military strategists of the countries that are refusing to kneel in front of the barbaric terror of the West, responsible for hundreds of millions of murders and billions of ruined lives, are planning how to defend their countries and the world.

Once again, the world is at work! It is building trenches, educating people, preparing them for the final showdown with the culture that has been tormenting our Planet for centuries.

It is the moment of great hope and renewed enthusiasm.

Of course, if seen from Western capitals,

everything is bleak and depressing. There is no 'hope' at all.

I agree fully: there is no hope 'for *them*'.

The logic, the 'philosophy' with which the Europeans and the North Americans have become accustomed to analyze the world, has arrived at a dead end.

Yes, it is 'the end of philosophy', or as they say, 'the end of history'. I fully agree: it is the end of *their* philosophy and of *their* history.

That's why, reading about *their* elections or statements produced by *their* politicians, is nothing less than a waste of time. The world realizes it, more and more.

Their 'new tricks' are actually very old. Their entire system is outdated. It should have been retired at least one hundred years ago. It survived only because of its savagery and cruelty. It will go soon, anyway.

These days, encountering people inhabiting the West is like encountering those zombies who were living in Nazi Germany during WWII. After the war was over, they were street walking for years, at least many of them, repeating the same refrains: "We didn't know!" "We never realized". The Nazi propaganda and the one, which has been used in the West and in the colonies (as Noam Chomsky and I defined in our book "*On Western Terrorism*"), are based on precisely the same roots, foundations and methods. Both are extremely effective, when it comes to the total brainwashing of the population.

To follow up the last chapter of the imperialist and turbo capitalist morass of the West is embarrassing and useless.

Both Europe and the United States are suffering from a series of devastating mental illnesses, as was defined by the great Swiss psychologist Carl Gustav Jung, right after WWII.

Getting too much involved in pathological behavior, constantly studying and analyzing it, could only break and deeply depress any healthy person's mind.

There is nothing more to understand. Hundreds of millions of victims in all parts of the world are speaking for themselves.

The only rational issue here is this: how to stop this horror, as soon as possible? How to allow humanity to return to its natural development and evolution patterns?

I don't believe in 'punishments' and 'trials' and other vehicles of intimidation and of spreading fear. I don't care whether the West will 'pay' for all that it has done to the world. I only want it to be stopped, once and for all.

I work very hard for it to be stopped.

So are others.

And the world is watching, and all of a sudden enjoying what it sees.

Suddenly more and more people are daring to laugh at the global regime. Of course not in Paris, London or New York (here they are scared and obedient, even more than before). But outside, yes!

People on all continents want to see and hear about what 'others do', what 'we do', not what the Empire and its mental conditions are producing.

They are laughing and waiting impatiently for what a new day, a new year will bring. They are waiting for the true new beginning to arrive.

March 24, 2017

14
World Is Burning – While Western Left Is Quarreling

It really is a shame, and it is tiring, but it is actually nothing new: there is now total disarray amongst those countless 'progressive' and 'semi-left' Western intellectuals, publications, movements and political parties.

Cowardice, bloated egos, lack of discipline and intellectual pettiness are often to blame, but that is not all.

It is now absolutely clear that the Western *left* lost patently and shamelessly. It has almost no power, it has no courage to fight or to take risks, and it counts on no real political following in Europe, North America, Australia or New Zealand. 'The masses', those proverbial 'oppressed masses', have lately been electing and voting in various semi-fascist populists, unapologetic right-wing demagogues, and mainstream pro-business brutes.

Entire Marxist 'theoretical certainties' have been collapsing in front of our eyes. Or at least they have been in the West.

***

To a great extent, what is now happening is absolutely natural. The European *left* betrayed as early as in the 1980's, by becoming too soft, too undisciplined, too cautious and too self- centered. It put pragmatism above the ideals. It rapidly adopted the lexicon of the liberal ideological establishment, complete with Western perceptions of *human rights*, *democratic principles* and *political correctness*. It ceased to be revolutionary; it essentially stopped all revolutionary activities, and it abandoned the core element of any true left-wing identity – internationalism.

Without at least some basic internationalist principles, the left is now essentially reduced to some sort of local trade union level: "Let us fight for better labor conditions and health care at home, and to hell with all that neo-colonialist plunder of the world which is expected to pay for almost all of our benefits. As long as we eat well and have long vacations, why should we rebel, why should we fight?"

The Western *left* has also failed to honestly address global history and especially the role which both Europe and North America have been playing in it. Many so-called 'progressive' Western thinkers have essentially adopted the imperialist rhetoric and revanchist interpretation of various key historic events, hence becoming 'anti-Communist' themselves.

After that, almost everything was lost, went down the drain.

Revolutionary flags were burned, at least metaphorically. Good old slogans were ditched. Then, instead of marches and violent demonstrations and clashes with the authorities representing the regime, increasingly comfortable couches in front of the latest high- definition television sets got quickly filled with millions of flabby over-indulgent bodies.

Now really ugly fights over the shrinking pie are raging. Theoretical Trotskyists and theoretical Maoists are at each other's throats. There are, of course, Leninists, and others, many others.

Things went much further, still: these days, in the West, most 'progressives' go 'by the issues', refusing to commit to anything greater, full-heartedly. This position is increasingly in vogue, and it essentially shouts: 'I have my own philosophy. I don't need any ideology at all.'

No revolution has ever been won like this. But in the West, there is no desire for true revolution. Belonging to *left* is mainly just a pose, with a social media account and a selfie. It is not serious, and it is not intended to be.

There are, of course, Anarcho-syndicalists with their air of superiority and lofty theories that would be out rightly rejected and laughed at by the great majority of the truly oppressed people in places like Asia or Africa.

Lately, I don't even know, anymore, who is who, in that small and petty world. I am not monitoring it, I hardly participate in theoretical discussions.

I write, using basically just two publications as my platform, from which my writing goes to the world, in various languages.

But that 'small and petty world' is obviously monitoring me. And what it sees, it does not like.

***

After launching with one of the mightiest [online left] publications in the West (I don't really want to name the publication, but my readers, most likely know which one I'm talking about) some 300 essays in the last 7 or 8 years, I was literally dumped by it at the very end of 2017. I will never find out the real reason, but most likely it was due to my 'too left wing' convictions, and too anti-Western, too open rhetoric. And yes, there was actually some hint: The editors did not like it that I write for 'Russian state-sponsored media', which in turn has some links to allegedly radical left-wing sites in the U.S.

In the eyes of the anti-Communist, 'we-go-by-the-issues' Western media, any 'state sponsored' or 'state controlled' media is *bad*, extremely bad!

Even if it belongs to those countries that are heroically fighting against Western imperialism, trying to save our Planet. Or perhaps it is considered *especially bad* if it belongs to such countries. It obviously applies to the Chinese, Russian, Venezuelan, Cuban, or Iranian media outlets. In summary – it applies to all media worldwide that are fighting to prevent the Western monstrous imperialist endgame from taking place; to the media that is fighting with force and zeal, and with (lately) tremendous success.

Instead of obediently waiting for the Western *right* or Western *left*, to define the world, now the Chinese, Russians, Latin Americans and the Middle Easterners are suddenly daring to re-define events that are taking place on this Planet. They are interviewing Westerners themselves, while holding a mirror to those monsters that became both the European and North American societies.

And instead of letting only Westerners speak, there are suddenly African, Asian, Russian, Arab and Latin American people appearing in front of the cameras.

Instead of that 'noble' "look what we are doing to the world", the true victims but also true revolutionaries are leading passionate debates.

Instead of some PhD professor in London debating whether China is truly Communist or not, it is now Chinese people speaking up, clarifying what their own country is and is not.

And the Western *left* does not like it. It is clear that it does not like such developments at all.

The Western *left* 'does not like any state-sponsored media'. It does not like it when others are speaking. Well, it may be even deeper than that: it appears that it does not really like anyone who is really fighting and who is winning: *it does not like the left that is actually holding power!*

Because the Western left is much more part of the *West* than of *the left*. Because deep down, it is comfortable, even obsessed with its exceptionalism.

Because despite those horrid centuries of colonialist and imperialist plunder of the world by Europe and North America, it does not truly believe that the crimes were committed *because* of Western culture and way of thinking.

Because, deep down, it really does not think that the non-Western nations and their media and thinkers are capable of defining and describing the world accurately, or even describing their own countries accurately. Non-Westerners simply cannot and should not be trusted. Only Western intellectuals have some sort of inherited right to make fully qualified decisions on such important topics as: whether China is Communist or not, whether Russia under President Putin is a progressive country or not, whether Iran is socialist or just a brutal religious state, whether Assad's government is 'legitimate', whether the North Korean leadership is 'insane' or whether President Maduro of Venezuela 'just went too far'.

As the world is finally preparing to defend itself against the inevitable Western aggressions, as the people of Asia, Russia, Latin America, Africa and the Middle East are discovering their own voices silenced for centuries by colonialist barbarity, as it is while the governments of these countries are making such discussion platforms possible, the Western *left* is howling at the moon, beating its chest in self-righteous narcissist gestures, and essentially insulting those who are fighting, standing tall, building much better world and yes – governing!

In several countries of South America, the left has recently been defeated precisely because it was too influenced 'ideologically' (or more precisely, 'anti-ideologically') by those weak, obsolete and overcautious Western pseudo-revolutionaries. Latin Americans should not, and hopefully will not, make similar mistakes in the future.

No revolutionary country can aim at perfection, yet. Revolution is not a bed of roses, said Fidel. Defending one's country against brutal foreign invasions is not always a pretty business: it is thoroughly messy and bloody stuff.

The weak and soft-skinned Western *left* can demand from non-Western revolutionary governments both 'purity' and a 'silk-gloved-approach', simply because it has no idea (or it doesn't care) what it is like to govern in countries consisting of millions of men, women and children who have been forced to live in absolute shit, after being robbed of everything by European and North American slave drivers. One simple mistake which those governments make, one sign of weakness, and their countries will go up in smoke, end up in ruins, in oblivion: like Iraq, like Afghanistan, like Yeltsin's Russia, or like China during the "century of humiliation".

***

The 'over-sensitivity' of the Western *left* is actually only a *façade*, it is not real.

Just as an example, the editors of the above-mentioned magazine, which has so unceremoniously stopped publishing my work, never showed any interest in my well-being or safety. I think if I would have dropped dead in one of the war zones I have covered, they'd hardly notice. Articles and essays signed by me would simply stop coming. Everyone is, after all, replaceable. To offer any support would be below their dignity. But to ask, regularly, for the reader's financial support, never has been.

The 'State-sponsored' media in the

revolutionary countries does treat their people differently. At least some of it does.

***

And quarreling goes on. I lost interest in the details. It is all time consuming and irrelevant.

In the meantime, I feel more and more comfortable writing for those new and proud media outlets, worldwide, edited far away from the West. I like it when my comrades are getting strong, when they are winning. I want them to govern and to govern well. And I want their countries to survive.

Things are that simple!

It is a great honor to show my films on *TeleSur* and *Al-Mayadeen*, to write for the *New Eastern Outlook*, *China Daily*, *Countercurrents*, and *Russia Today*. I enjoy appearing live, regularly, on *PressTV*.

I feel that each word that I write and utter through those media outlets are intended for my friends, for my comrades, for our struggle and for a much better world.

And let me repeat: I want my friends and comrades to win, to succeed, and yes, to govern! The Western *left* can keep quarreling, chewing itself: *'Who said what? Who is real left and who is not? Who is pure Marxist and who is simply some social democrat?"*

Not all Western *left* media outlets are as described above. There are still some wonderful writers and editors in the West, too. But the overall situation in Europe and North America is deteriorating.

The governing and struggling revolutionary and internationalist left in the independent countries does not usually have time for lofty debates. We have Moscow, Beijing, Caracas, Havana, La Paz, Damascus and many other wonderful cities behind our backs – to defend. We will deal with the theory later, much later, after we win, after there is real peace, accompanied by justice, after all of us on this planet can proudly be what we really are – ourselves and defined by ourselves!

February 3, 2018

15
Only Rational Thinking Will Save The World

Scenario ONE: Imagine that you are on board a ship, which is slowly sinking. There is no land in sight, and your radio transmitter is not functioning properly. There are several people on board and you care for them, deeply. You don't want this to be the end of 'everything'.

What do you do?

A) You fix for yourself a nice portion of fried rice with prawns
B) You turn on the TV set, which is still somehow miraculously working, and watch the news about the future Scottish

referendum or on BREXIT

C) You jump into the water immediately, try to identify the damage, and then attempt to do something unthinkable with your simple tools and capabilities: to save the ship

Imagine another scenario:

SCENARIO TWO: By mistake, your wife eats two full tubes of sleeping pills, supposedly confusing them with a new line of candies. As you find her on the floor, she appears to be unconscious and her face looks rather bluish.

What would your course of action be?

A) After you realize that her high heels do not match the color of her pantyhose, you run to the closet in search of a much better pair of shoes to achieve the balance

B) You carry her without delay to the bathroom, pump out her stomach, and try to resuscitate her while calling the ambulance using the speakerphone function

C) You recall how you first met, get

nostalgic, and rush to your living room library in order to find a book of love sonnets by Pablo Neruda, which you then recite to her kneeling on the carpet

Now brace yourself for a great surprise. Unless you choose C) for scenario one, and B) for scenario two, you can actually consider yourself absolutely "normal" by most North American and European standards.

However, if you opt for C) or B) respectively, you could easily pass off for an extremist, a radical and ideological left-wing fanatic.

***

The West has brought the world to the brink of total collapse, but its citizens, even its intellectuals, are stubbornly refusing to grasp the urgency. Like ostriches, many are hiding their heads in the sand. Others are behaving like a surgeon who opts for treating a small cut on a finger of his patient who is actually dying from a terrible gunshot wound.

There seems to be an acute lack of rational thinking, and especially of people's ability to grasp the proportions of global occurrences and events. For years I have been arguing that destroying the ability to compare and to see things from the universal perspective has been one of the most successful endeavors of the Western indoctrination drive (dispersed through education, media/disinformation and 'culture'). It has effectively influenced and pacified both, the people in the West itself, and those living in its present and former colonies (particularly the local 'elites' and their offspring).

There seems to be no capacity to compare and consistently analyze, for instance, those certainly unsavory but mainly defensive actions taken by the revolutionary governments and countries, with the most horrid and appalling crimes committed by the colonialist regimes of the West all over Asia, Latin America, the Middle East and Africa, which took place in approximately the same historical era.

It is not only history that is seen in the West through totally crooked and 'out of focus' lenses, it is also the present, which has been perceived and 'analyzed' in an out of context way and without applying hardly any rational comparisons. Rebellious and

212

independent-minded countries in Asia, Latin America, Africa and the Middle East (most of them have been actually forced to defend themselves against the extremely brutal attacks and subversion campaigns administered by the West) have been slammed, even in the so-called 'progressive' circles of the West, with much tougher standards than those that are being applied towards both Europe and North America, two parts of the world that have been continuously spreading terror, destruction and unimaginable suffering among the people inhabiting all corners of the globe.

Most crimes committed by the left-wing revolutions were in direct response to invasions, subversions, provocations and other attacks coming from the West. Almost all the most terrible crimes committed by the West were committed abroad, and were directed against enslaved, exploited, thoroughly plundered and defenseless people in almost all parts of the world.

Now, according to many, the endgame is approaching. Rising oceans are swallowing entire countries, as I witnessed in several parts of Oceania. It is a horrid, indescribable sight!

People in numerous countries governed by pro-Western regimes are shedding millions of their inhabitants, while some nations are basically ceasing to exist, like Papua or Kashmir, to give just two obvious examples.

The environment is thoroughly ruined where the 'lungs' of the world used to work hard, just a few decades ago, making our planet healthy.

Tens of millions of people are now on the move, their countries thoroughly ruined by Western geopolitical games. Instead of influencing and helping to guide humanity, such great cultures as those of Iraq, Afghanistan and Syria are now forced to disgorge millions of desperate refugees. They are barely surviving, humiliated and hardly relevant.

Extremist religious groups (of all faiths, and definitely not only belonging to the Muslim religion) are being groomed by the Western Machiavellian ideologues and strategists, then dispersed to all corners of the globe: South Asia, the Middle East, China, Latin America, Africa, and even

Oceania.

It is a total disgrace what imperialism has managed to reduce our humanity to.

Most of the world is actually trying to function 'normally', 'democratically', following its natural instincts, which are based on simple humanism. But it is being constantly derailed, attacked and tormented by the brutal monstrous and merciless hydra – the Western expansionism and its 'culture' or nihilism, greed, cynicism and slavery.

It is so obvious where we are going as a human race.

We want to fly, we want freedom and optimism and beauty to govern our lives. We want to dream and to create something deep, meaningful, happy and kind. But there are those horrible weights hanging from our feet. There are chains restraining our actions. There is constant fear, which is making us betray all our ideals, as well as each other, again and again; fear that makes us, humans, act like shameless cowards and egoists. As a result we are not flying, we are only crawling, and not even forward, but in bizarre, irrational ellipses and circles.

Still, I do not believe that the endgame is inevitable!

***

For many years I have been sending warnings, I have been writing and showing and presenting thousands of terrible images of destruction, of the irreversible collapse, of barbarity.

I have generally kept nothing to myself. I have recycled my work, my films and books, into new journeys into the darkest abysses of our world. I have received hardly any support from the outside world. But I couldn't stop: what I have been witnessing, the danger to the planet and total devastation, have forced me to never give up the struggle. If necessary and most of the time, I have done it alone. I spent too much time in Latin America; I could not give up. I learned too much from Cuba and so many other wonderful places; I felt I had no right to surrender.

Whenever the horrors from which our planet is suffering would overwhelm me, I'd 'collapse', as I did last year. Then I'd bury myself somewhere for a short period of time, collect myself together, get up and continue with my work and my struggle. I have never ceased to trust people. Some would come full of initial enthusiasm, offering much, then betray me, and leave. Still, I have never lost faith in human beings. This year, instead of slowing down, I 'adopted' one more place, which is in agony – Afghanistan.

My only request, my only demand has been, that the world listens, that it sees, that it tries to comprehend, before it is too late. This request of mine has proven to be, I realize now, too 'demanding', and too 'radical'.

Sometimes I ask: have I achieved much? Have I opened many eyes? Have I managed to build many bridges between the different struggling parts of the world? As an internationalist I have to question my own actions, my effectiveness.

I have to admit, honestly: I don't know the answers to my own questions. But I keep working and struggling.

***

The world looks different if observed

and analyzed from a pub in Europe or North America, or if you are actually standing on one of those atolls in the middle of the South Pacific (Oceania) that are under the constant assault of tidal waves, dotted with dead stumps of palm trees pointing accusatively towards the sky. These islets are at the forefront of the battle for the survival of our planet, and they are obviously losing.

Everything also appears to be much more urgent but also 'real', when observed from the black and desolate plains of the hopelessly logged out Indonesian islands of Borneo/Kalimantan and Sumatra.

I used to recount in my essays, just for my readers to know, what the villages somewhere like Goma in the Democratic Republic of Congo (DRC), look and feel like, after the murderous assaults by the pro-Rwandese, and therefore pro-Western, militias. It was important for me to explain how things are 'right in the middle of it', on the ground. I used to write about mass rapes and mutilations, about the burning flesh, terrible torture... I stopped some time ago. You at least once witness all this or you simply didn't. If you did then you know what it all looks like, what it feels like and smells like... or you could never imagine it, no matter how many books and reports you read, no matter how many images you consume.

I have been trying to speak about all this to the people in the West, at conferences, universities, or even through my films and books. They do listen, mostly respectfully. They do show politely how outraged and 'horrified' they are (it is 'expected' of them). Some say: 'I want to do something'. Most of them do absolutely nothing, but even if they decide to take action, it is usually for themselves, just to feel good, to feel better, to convince their own conscience that they have actually 'done at least something for the humanity'.

I used to blame them. I don't, anymore. This is how the world is arranged. However, I have sharply reduced my work-visits to both North America and Europe. I don't feel that I click with the people in those places. We don't think the same way, we don't feel the same, and even our logic and rationale are diametrically different.

My recent three-week stay in Europe clearly revealed to me, how little there is in common between the West's state of mind and the reality in which the great majority of the world has been living.

***

In the past, before the Western empires and the sole "Empire" took most of determination and enthusiasm away from the people, the most talented of human beings used to make no distinction between their personal lives, their creativity and their relentless work and duty towards humanity.

In several places including Cuba, it is how many people still live.

In the West, everyone and everything is now fragmented and life itself became objectively meaningless: there is distinct time to work (satisfying one's personal career, guaranteeing survival, advancing 'prestige' and ego), there is time to play, and for family life... and there is occasionally time to think about humanity or, very rarely, about the survival of our planet.

Needless to say, this selfish approach has failed in helping to advance the world.

It has also squarely failed when it comes to stopping at least some of the monstrosities committed by Western imperialism.

When I go to the opera house or some great classical music concert, it is in order to get some deep inspiration, to get fired up about my work, to recycle the beauty that I'm expressing in my novels and films, theatre plays and even political reports. I never go to get simply 'entertained'. It is never for my own needs only.

It is also essential for me to work closely with the people that I love, including my own mother who is already 82 years old.

It is because I know there is absolutely no time to waste. And also because everything is and should be intertwined in life: love, work, duty, and the struggle for the survival and progress of our world.

***

I may be labeled as a fanatic, but I am decisively choosing those C) and B) options from the 'dilemmas' I depicted above.

I am choosing rationality, now that the US 'armada' packed with the nuclear weapons is sailing towards both China and

North Korea, now that the Tomahawk missiles have rained down on Syria, now that the West will be sending thousands more mercenaries to one of the most devastated countries on Earth - Afghanistan.

Survival and then the advancement of the world should be our greatest goal. I believe it and I stand by it. In time of absolute crises, which we are experiencing right now, it is irresponsible, almost grotesque, to simply 'continue to live our daily lives'.

Imperialism has to be stopped, once and for all, by all means. At the moment when the survival of humanity is at stake, the end justifies all means. Or as the motto of Chile goes: "By Reason Or By Force".

Of course, if those 'who know' do not act, if they are cowardly and opportunistically do nothing, from a universal perspective, nothing much will happen: one small planet in one of the so many galaxies will simply cease to exist. Most likely there are many inhabited planets in the universe, many civilizations.

However, I happen to love this world and this particular Planet. I know it well, from the Southernmost tip all the way to the north. I know its deserts and valleys, mountains and oceans, its marvelous and touching creatures, its great cities as well as god-forsaken villages. I know its people. They have many faults; and much that could be condemned in them, and much that should be improved. But I still believe that there is more that could be admired in them than denounced.

Now it is time to think, rationally and quickly, and then to act. No small patches will do, no 'feel good' actions. Only a total reset, overhaul. Call it the Revolution if you will, or simply C) and B). No matter how you define it, it would have to come rapidly, very rapidly, or there soon will be nothing to love, to defend, and to work for, anymore.

April 14, 2017

16
Why I Reject Western Courts and Justice

There is a small courthouse from the 'British era', standing right in the center of Hong Kong. It is neat, well-built, remarkably organized and some would even say – elegant.

Earlier this year I visited there with an Afghan-British lawyer, who had been touring East Asia for several months. Hong Kong was her last destination; afterwards she was planning to return home to London. The Orient clearly confused and overwhelmed her, and no matter how 'anti-imperialist' she tried to look, most of her references were clearly going back to the adoptive homeland – the United Kingdom.

"It looks like England," she exclaimed when standing in the middle of Hong Kong.

There was clearly excitement and nostalgia in her voice.

To cheer her up even more, I took her to the courthouse. My good intentions backfired: as we were leaving, she uttered words that I expected but also feared for quite some time:

"You know, there are actually many good things that can be said about the British legal system."

***

I thought about that short episode in Hong Kong now, as I drove all around her devastated country of childhood, Afghanistan. As always, I worked without protection, with no bulletproof vests, armored vehicles or military escorts, just with my Afghan driver who doubled as my interpreter and also as my friend. It was Ramadan and to let him rest, I periodically got behind the wheel. We were facing countless detentions, arrests and interrogations by police, military and who knows what security forces, but we were moving forward, always forward, despite all obstacles.

From that great distance, from the heights of the mountains of Afghanistan, the courthouse in Hong Kong kept falling into proportion and meaningful perspective.

It was surrounded by an enormous city, once usurped and sodomized by the British Crown. A city where 'unruly locals' were being killed, tortured, flogged and regularly imprisoned.

And it was not only Hong Kong that has suffered: the entire enormous country of China with one of the oldest and greatest cultures on Earth had been brutally ransacked, including its splendid capital – Beijing – that was invaded and almost totally destroyed by the French and British troops. For a long period, China was divided, humiliated, impoverished and tormented.

But the courthouse, a little neat temple of colonialist justice, now stood in the middle of the once occupied city, whispering about the days when it offered certainty and pride to all those who came to Hong Kong as colonizers, as well as to all those who served and licked the boots of their British masters.

The courthouse was providing confidence to people who were longing for one, just as they did during the grotesque and perverse days, as well as now.

Behind its walls ruled clearly defined and meticulously obeyed spirit of fairness: if one's chicken got slaughtered, or if one's tricycle god smashed by a hammer of a mad shopkeeper, the legendary British justice was administered promptly and properly.

Some people would argue, of course, that the entire colonialism was unjust, that the killing of tens of millions of people in Asia, Africa, the Middle East and elsewhere was much more noteworthy than settling fairly and justly some domestic or real estate dispute. Such voices, however, have been always quickly silenced, or bought (with money, diplomas, or other means).

Certainly, the British Crown has been busy subjugating entire countries and continents, murdering innocent people, freely plundering and enslaving men, women and children. Tens of millions died in the British-triggered famines alone, on the Sub-Continent and elsewhere. But that was done "outside" the legal framework, and it was never fit to be discussed publicly in a 'polite society', by both the English people as well as by the émigré elites.

Now the UK has been absorbed by the 'great' Western Empire, governed by its offspring. Global genocides continue to murder millions. For those, no one gets punished, while the fines for speeding or not wearing seat belts are getting transparently dispersed among the servile citizens of the British Isles.

You kick your dog in public, and you could get arrested, then fined, or perhaps even thrown into jail. You shout at your girlfriend, she runs to police, and they open a 'criminal investigation' against you.

You shoot a few missiles at some independent country, killing dozens of innocent people, and it is business as usual. You overthrow some 'unruly' African government, and no court of justice, local or international, would even bother to hear the case against you, properly and seriously.

Alexander Thomson from 'UK Column News' in the UK, commented for this essay:

"British justice is fine for peer-to-peer disputes such as breakages and traffic accidents. You'll most likely get a fair hearing. But at the macro level? The British and their offspring have pillaged entire continents. Where's the justice there? If there's none but "victors' justice", should that legal system be honored by the nations of the world?"

I often wonder whether even the British citizens themselves should honor such a charade?

***

International criminal attorney Christopher Black spoke to the press after joining Rwandans and Congolese to present their complaint against Paul Kagame at the ICC. (Source: beforeitsnews.com)

The renowned Canadian international lawyer Christopher Black, has doubts about the entire international legal system which is literally dictated by Western countries, predominantly by the US and UK. He wrote for this essay:

"Instead of peaceful and mutually respectful relations between nations, adherence to the fundamental principles of the peaceful resolution of conflicts and disagreements between nations set out in the UN Charter, of the principles of the Non-Aligned Movement, the world is faced with ultimatums, bribes, threats and assault. Their brutality would be unimaginable if it was not so routine."

The question is: should the legal system, which coerces dozens of countries all over the world, be taken seriously, even respected? Isn't it ridiculous, even debauched, to honor the US and British courts, considering that they are serving the most aggressive and morally defunct system in the world?

Christopher Black continues:

"The most important question that arises from the discussion of how to establish a just world in which every nation has equal rights and status, in which national sovereignty is respected and the peaceful resolution of international issues as a matter of course is what type of legal mechanisms and structures need to be established in order to achieve and maintain this equilibrium.

It is not a simple matter since laws and legal structures reflect the socio-economic structure of a society. This necessarily creates a conflict between different socio-economic and legal systems that is difficult to resolve. The legal systems of socialist societies with their emphasis on socio-economic protection and support of the workers, are completely different from those of the capitalist societies, in which the central role of law is to protect private property and ease the flow of capital, in opposition to the interests of the workers. This creates conflict between nations with different socio-economic systems..."

It is a well-known fact that those systems that are antagonistic to the Western dictates get routinely attacked, even destroyed. Right now several countries are under direct attack from the West: from Venezuela to Syria, to name just two victims out of dozens.

On closer examination, it is all nothing more than a 'mafia justice', or call it a terror.

***

I refuse to respect such a system, including its courts and its entire farce called 'justice'. To me, it is all 'illegal' and corrupt. If confronted, I'd refuse to accept the authority of the Western legal system; I'd just laugh in the faces of its judges.

Lawyers serving such a system are, at least from my personal point of view, nothing more than collaborators or at least –spineless gold-diggers.

During the Nazi era in Germany, family or real estate disputes were resolved fairly and briskly. However, that doesn't mean that Slavs, Roma, Jews, or non-white people should have had any respect for the German 'justice' of these years.

Certainly, your goat could be avenged if slaughtered illegally, but the next day, no one would save you from going up in smoke from the chimney of a concentration camp crematorium.

From the heights of totally destroyed and miserable mountain villages in Afghanistan, all this is suddenly clear and 'obvious'.

It is also very clear when observed from Syria or Latin America, or the Democratic Republic of Congo, where of course almost no Westerner would bother to travel.

Christopher Black concludes:

"Attempts to establish a world order in

which a dialogue of civilizations is the norm instead of conflict between civilizations are foundering on a crude return to a "might makes right" attitude against which any attempt to insist on adherence to international law and norms, even common morality, is viewed as a weakness to be exploited.

The question therefore arises as to how nations and peoples can establish the necessary legal mechanisms to survive and flourish when there exist those who oppose any such mechanisms being established and act to destroy the mechanisms that do exist. The answer is to take the power from those who want this unjust world order, this world for the criminals. We know what is to be done. But that is not good enough. We have to determine how it is to be done."

The first step is, surely, to refuse this criminal 'justice' system, even to mock it, and ridicule it.

To serve criminals is a crime itself. To legitimize this illegitimate system by pretending that justice could be served inside its frame is itself immoral.

A courthouse in Hong Kong is not a

temple of fairness. To pretend that it is would be a cynical mockery, a 'spit in the face' to millions of those who lost their lives in China and all over the world, at the hands of the British and Western colonizers.

And one more comment about Western justice: if just slightly exaggerating, one could easily arrive to the conclusion that in a world ruled by brutal and unbridled imperialism, the only honorable place to dwell in is jail!

June 23, 2017

17
Love vs Pornography, Revolution vs Passivity

Y ou say that you want facts – facts and more facts, before you can commit. Before you finally decide to become part of something: a political party, a movement or another human being. You already have plenty of them: an avalanche, a tsunami of facts. "In fact", your life is overflowing with facts. Most of them are brought directly to your living room or bedroom, or to your office; they shine from the liquid crystals of your computer monitors, and from increasingly flat and sleek television screens.

There is really no need to travel, is there? There is no need to "get dirty". Without leaving your chair or couch, you can even get some basic science of Newton,

Einstein or Leonardo da Vinci. You can experience, second-hand of course, but in the safety and comfort of your home, the most extreme misery of Haitian or Jamaican slums. You can be shown a battleground, you can see the most exotic and most 'forbidden' women being made love to by someone else, and you can get inside royal palaces.

It is all there, at your fingertips: formulas and definitions, music and porn, history and even some poetry, if poetry is what you are really searching for.

There is no reason to step outside. Of course many people have to go out, at least from Monday to Friday, to attend to their typically monotonous jobs. From time to time they have to buy some groceries, although groceries can be ordered online or using the phone, and some jobs these days do not even require the personal presence of employees.

While individualism (egoism) is what increasingly defines most of the cultures in the West, true individuality (uniqueness) has almost vanished.

Although the internet is overflowing with information, data and "facts", although there are now hundreds of channels available from the menus of television cable providers, the *living room – computer* or *living room – television set* combinations are producing increasingly monotonous results: people are more and more phlegmatic, their way of thinking is uniformed, and they are not willing to take almost any risks: intellectually, emotionally or physically.

Passivity is being constantly rationalized, defended. On the surface, reasons given to justify lack of commitment are logical, 'sensible', and sometimes even righteous.

Passivity has become 'calm', and so have despair, desolation and gloom.

Instead of encouraging violent rebellious outbursts of anguish as something natural, positive and even essential (should one not be fighting with all his or her might against all the forces which are making life pointless and useless?), almost everything that is defined by society as "negative emotions" gets subdued and controlled by medication and therapy. This way, medical "science" becomes a culprit, murders many healthy reactions, and in the end, kills life itself.

While individualism (egoism) is what increasingly defines most of the cultures in the West, true individuality (uniqueness) has almost vanished. Although the internet is overflowing with information, data and "facts", although there are now hundreds of channels available from the menus of television cable providers, the living room – computer or living room – television set combinations are producing increasingly monotonous results: people are more and more phlegmatic, their way of thinking is uniformed, and they are not willing to take almost any risks: intellectually, emotionally or physically.

It is rarely pronounced, but it is essential to realize: A person who feels violently sick because he or she is surrounded by a thoroughly unhealthy, even insane environment (political system, family, work, sets of constantly repeated lies) is actually reacting in a vigorous and healthy way. It is like when the body is fighting against severe infection. Only in this case, the battle is mental.

People are expected to be "normal", while standards defining "normalcy" have roots in mental illnesses from which entire society is clearly suffering. Not only immigrants; now everyone is obliged to "conform". What does it really mean, to conform? Is it: to become atomized, apathetic and therefore alone and vulnerable? Life then flows slowly, calmly, coldly and emotionlessly. A person grows up, matures, ages and dies. Society slowly deteriorates. Planet Earth is getting gradually ruined.

Surrounded by uniformed and perpetual misery, passivity and amnesia, one is not aware of his or her suffering. The screen in front of people shines late into the night. Everything is reduced to short barks and uniformed symbols pre- programmed into mobile phones.

Something has gone missing. There seems to be an urgent lack of something very essential, a gaping deficit. In such an environment, love cannot thrive, and revolution can never take place. In sterility and surrounded by emotional emptiness, human beings can live a little bit longer, but can such an existence be really called life?

Reality is "authentic" only if experienced holistically and first-hand. This is the conclusion at which I arrived, after witnessing hundreds of conflicts all over the world, but also after observing so many glorious moments, so many great human achievements, in virtually all corners of the globe.

A computer monitor only offers extremely filtered, even "censored" images of reality (no matter how high-definition it might be), as well as some basic sound. Even our imperfect and limited human senses are capable of capturing, registering and processing incomparably much more than that.

When relying exclusively on processed and filtered reality (images and sound), a great part of our mind gets dormant, it begins to deteriorate (even degenerate), and eventually the process becomes irreversible. It is as if you only had use of your right hand for almost your entire life, no legs and no left hand: the situation would most definitely lead to the weakening of muscles and to fatal physical deformities. The same happens with the human mind, with the brain, if it is prevented from performing all of its natural functions on a regular basis.

I insist that "knowledge" and "understanding of reality" has to consist of a "complete approach", in which, at least most of our senses, are involved. Practically: to 'truly comprehend' requires "being there".

Let me give you one example, just one, although there are of course thousands of paradigms that I could provide:

You can sit all your life in Berlin, London or Boston, and watch news on your television screen, you can mull over countless "facts" provided by your best friends (internet and smart phone) but you would never, ever come close to understanding what has been happening during the last two decades in Latin America, or what is happening in Syria right now.

To understand, you'd have to roll up your sleeves, stop vegetating and begin living. You'd have to experience, with all your senses, what the dampness coming from the walls in tropical slums some fifteen or twenty years ago felt like, you'd have to observe from miserable and over-populated hills those obnoxiously expensive condominiums on the horizon, you'd have to smell bad breath of young women who couldn't afford dental care while the country was awash with petrodollars. You'd have to see young people dance, on Friday nights, so desperately and hopelessly. One evening you'd have to walk down some narrow alley, alone, and see two men with guns walking straight towards you. You'd have to smell the cheap perfume of a woman approaching you at two in the morning in a dive frequented by local journalists, grabbing you by the shoulders, beginning to sob, confessing that now she is a prostitute, but just one year ago she was an elementary school teacher and wanted to live in a little house with a neat and colorful garden. You'd have to know how stale the air used to be in rooms stuffed with bodies in some godforsaken public hospital where poor people were dying from cancer. You'd have to see and feel and smell more, much more, in order to understand why those of us who were there then, are still where we are now, fully determined and loyal, working and living for the Revolution.

Ernesto *Che* Guevara had to leave his provincial bubble of family, which consisted of doctors enjoying their upper middle-class life; he had to hit the road. In a way, he never returned. *Che* had to see and smell and feel, in order to get engaged, to take sides, to become committed; he had to understand what misery is, what leprosy is, what hunger and despair are, but also, he had to face all that tremendous glory of his continent, of South America.

It all goes hand in hand: in order to fight, to commit, to risk your life, you have to love, or at least you have to know how to love. In order to love, first you have to be alive!

During his endless motorcycle journey through the continent, what *Che* experienced was not necessarily something "factual", or even "rational".

What Venezuelan revolutionaries based their actions on a few decades later was mainly deeply emotional. Their feelings eventually got rationalized, leading to the pledge to liberate the continent. The next step was to take several determined actions. Facts were employed, too, but they were harvested strictly for the Cause, for the Revolution. It was not, and it was never meant to be, the other way around.

Revolution is an highly emotional event, and so is love, so is life. There is no life and there is no love without rebellion, without "private revolution", without commitment. To live and to love requires courage and personal freedom, but it also requires full dedication and loyalty, self-sacrifice and determination.

During the Revolution, as well as when one is in love, all senses are involved. One is fighting for humanity. One is fighting for happiness of his or her other half. No matter what obstacles are blocking the way, no matter how hard the journey is, while loving or struggling, but especially while loving *and* struggling, a person is fully alive. Then and only then, his or her life gains meaning.

Revolution can be totally stripped of religion; it could be, and it often is, completely secular. But it always relies, significantly, on three brilliant Muses, three sisters, that are never far away from anything great that is moving our human race forward. Their names are Faith, Love and Hope.

Faith can be never based on facts. Love can be never based on facts. Hope is not based on facts. The three sisters cannot be 'studied', and not much can be learned about them from the internet. They could never be fully understood with logic. All three of them simply represent Life.

Life that is increasingly absent from societies that are controlling the world; societies which are more and more limiting the natural range of human senses, while herding men and women into dark and narrow pre-fabricated tunnels that lead only into perverse meaninglessness.

Such societies have already managed to create a new horrible religion, a new breed of extreme fanaticism, based on cold, emotionless, and nonsensical "rationalism", on dehumanized "science", and on a pre-selected medley of "facts". Such societies have already choked to death both poetry and the human ability to dream. They have ended up raping the world, inseminating it with passivity and depression, forcing humanity to reject faith, love, and hope, to spit at commitments, at loyalty, at courage, at constructive and positive actions, at Life itself.

***

"Fact-based" virtual analyses of the world lead mostly to dark pessimism and negativism. It is not only because the prolonged staring at computer and television screens is depressing and unhealthy, but also since such analyses are to a great extent, "unreal" and deceiving.

The analogy to "'facts'-based virtual experience' versus 'beneficial human knowledge' would be: 'pornography' versus 'love'.

To a poet, to a revolutionary, to a dreamer, to a humanist, such knowledge that consists exclusively of 'hard facts' (spiced with countless formulas and test results) would appear as cold, absurd and as empty as 'hard porn'.

Love is not just the physical friction of two sexual organs, but also of great tenderness, compassion, honesty, and the disappearance of all fears accumulated throughout one's entire life. It is genuine liberation and great adventure, a "private revolution", a process through which the entire world, in fact the entire universe is re-discovered and re- defined, thoroughly and from the beginning, by two people, together.

True and big loves, like those loves that people used to experience and then write about in the past, (but so rarely now), were never easy, as people are not some simple beings, and two of them can hardly ever "perfectly match". There were almost always some big dramas and temporary breakouts, then passionate reunions; there were misunderstandings and even severe pain. It always required great determination and willpower for two strong individuals to remain together, to survive as a couple, as one unit.

It is always easier to give up, to leave, as is done these days. It is all down to those "facts" stripped of passion, depth and courage, isn't it?

Take a woman you think you fell in love with, and look at the facts – analyze her. Go ahead – try. Do it the way everything is done these days: coldly and rationally. Is she "good for you"? Is living with her going to "improve your life"? Aren't her buttocks too wide or legs bit too short? Isn't she a bit "complicated", in fact, "isn't she *too* complicated?" And, "doesn't she come with too much baggage?" Isn't being with her going to "jeopardize your career?" "Is it going to strain the relationship with your family?"

Such thoughts would have been considered grotesque in the past. But they are acceptable, even normal, now. And the conclusions are usually predictable: "if it is not easy, leave! Just go..."

Do you remember the greatest novel written by Hemingway: *"For Whom The Bell Tolls"*?

A man, a middle-class American teacher goes to Spain. He volunteers; he wants to fight on the side of socialism, on the side of Republican Spain, against fascism. His name is Robert Jordan. He meets a girl; her name is Maria. Maria's head was shaved, before she was brutally raped by fascist troops. From the beginning, it appears to be an absolutely impossible love, but to hell with it: it *is* love, and both Robert Jordan and Maria know it, they feel it, and they don't even attempt to be rational about it. Against all odds, suddenly but fully, two people from two faraway countries do give their lives to each other, and then they make love, and 'the earth moves', as it moves only once in a lifetime. And Maria dies, and Robert Jordan does not leave; he stays by the side of the road, in a futile but heroic gesture, waiting for a fascist column to approach, so he could do what he pledged to do, to her and to himself: to fight and most likely to die in this foreign land, to die honestly, for Maria's country.

Well, this is how people used to write, and this is how they use to live... and this is how they used to love. This is what used to be *normal*, and what used to be admired and treasured.

And this is still how I write and live and love, and I don't give a damn whether it is in vogue or not. I know when I write well, no matter what others say. I know when I fight bravely and honestly, even if, at the end, I lose. One knows these things, as one perhaps also knows when he or she lives like a coward, or when he or she betrays. I also know when 'the earth moves', and if it does, even if the other one does something insane and 'unforgivable', no matter what I declare, I will stay.

In today's world, Maria and women like Maria would be seen as very 'bad match'. An injured, traumatized woman with 'terrible baggage' carried on her shoulders.

No 'sane man' would take her hand. No one would embrace her; no one would fight and die for her. (Although somewhere deep inside I know: I would... I am... even now.)

Pornography, or some secret encounter with a bimbo in a love hotel, would be much 'safer', much 'simpler' for today's 'sensible' Western men.

That is why, I'm convinced, in such an environment, with such a state of mind, no true revolution is possible anymore!

***

Every great love is confusing and often painful. True revolutions are never tidy, never easy, and never faultless. It is because both human love and human passion for progress and change consists of a set of complex emotions and instincts, sometimes clashing, often co-existing somehow inharmoniously, but always creating great whirlpool of passions, which actually makes life worth living.

By definition, love can never be 'sterile', and the same can be said about true revolution. True love and true revolution are always raw, full of fluids, of boiling blood, of tears. They consist of hope, of pain, but also of great joy.

Pornography is totally sterile, and sterile is that self-righteous universe of detachment, of cold 'impartial' observation of the world, as well as electronically transmitted "facts". Sterile is also the refusal to get 'engaged', to get 'dirty', to get involved, and to take sides. Sterile is not to fight and not to be ready to die for one's ideals.

Sterile is when one is desiring absolute purity: "I cannot get involved, because I'm not ready to fully support this ideal, this ideology, this revolution."

When I hear this, I immediately imagine those bodies of women, created by fashion and advertisement agencies: "perfect", smooth, slim, and tall... but absolutely lacking life and individuality.

I'm not attracted to such bodies, and I'm not attracted to 'perfect', tidy and 'inoffensive', 'harmless' ideologies. I'd never want to be with a woman whom I wouldn't want to murder, at least once. I'd never fight for perfection, only for human beings, and those are never thoroughly (and luckily) faultless.

During a revolution and also when one loves and is loved madly, one can easily burn to ashes, but that's life and it is better to go this way, than vanishing from influenza, old age or in a car accident.

One can also fall, disappear, while searching for true knowledge, because knowledge is often hidden in the most peculiar, dangerous and unsavory places. You have to come close, damn close, if you want to truly comprehend.

Sometimes, if you come too close, you die. But that is life, too. That's how it is and that's how it should be. Without tremendous effort, without true courage, stamina, passion, without taking risks, life is never worth living.

May 19, 2017

About Author

Philosopher, novelist, filmmaker, investigative journalist, poet, playwright, and photographer, Andre Vltchek is a revolutionary, internationalist and globetrotter. In all his work, he confronts Western imperialism and the Western regime imposed on the world.

He has covered dozens of war zones and conflicts from Iraq and Peru to Sri Lanka, Bosnia, Rwanda, Syria, DR Congo and Timor-Leste.

His latest books are *The Great October Socialist Revolution: Impact on the World and Birth of Internationalism*, *Exposing Lies of the Empire*, *Fighting Against Western Imperialism* and *On Western Terrorism* with Noam Chomsky.

Aurora and *Point of No Return* are his major work of fiction, written in English. *Nalezeny* is his novel written in Czech. Other works include a book of political non-fiction, *Western Terror: From Potosi to Baghdad* and *Indonesia: Archipelago of Fear,* also *Exile* (with Pramoedya Ananta Toer, and Rossie Indira) and *Oceania – Neocolonialism, Nukes & Bones.*

His plays are *'Ghosts of Valparaiso'* and *'Conversations with James'.*

He is a member of Advisory Committee of the BRussells Tribunal.

The investigative work of Andre Vltchek appears in countless publications worldwide.

Andre Vltchek has produced and directed several documentary films for the left-wing South American television network teleSUR. They deal with diverse topics, from Turkey/Syria to Okinawa, Kenya, Egypt and Indonesia, but all expose the effects of Western imperialism on the Planet. His feature documentary film *'Rwanda Gambit'* has been broadcasted by Press TV, and aims at reversing the official narrative on the 1994 genocide, as well as exposing the Rwandan and Ugandan plunder of DR Congo on behalf of Western imperialism. He produced the feature length documentary film about the Indonesian massacres of 1965 in *'Terlena – Breaking of The Nation'*, as well as in his film about the brutal Somali refugee camp, Dadaab, in Kenya: *'One Flew Over Dadaab'*. His Japanese crew filmed his lengthy discussion with Noam Chomsky on the state of the world, which is presently being made into a film.

He frequently speaks at revolutionary meetings, as well as at the principal universities worldwide.

He presently lives in Asia and the Middle East.

Website: http://andrevltchek.weebly.com/

Twitter: @AndreVltchek

THE GREAT OCTOBER SOCIALIST REVOLUTION:
Impact on the world and Birth of Internationalism

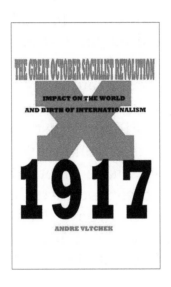

Powerful, Urgent, this book is straightforwardly challenging Western Anti-Communist and Anti-Internationalist Dogmas. "The Great October Socialist Revolution" began by a proud salvo from Aurora. It broke the prison wall as well as chains, and a secret road suddenly opened. The journey began. Several countries rode, following the revolutionary ideals. Since

then, some have fallen. Others rose again.

***

"Vltchek's book celebrates one of the most important events in modern political history a hundred years after it happened. The October Revolution in Russia challenged old authority structures, tyrannical beliefs and assumptions and started the anti-imperialist struggle on a global scale that continues to this day. Some countries have fallen despite trying to preserve their socialist ideals, Vltchek writes, while others have risen.

The West has been hostile to October and the ripples of liberation it created, since day one. The reactionary NATO alliance is still committed against such effects a hundred years later. Useful when confronted with the spike in hateful rhetoric and accusations coming out of Western capitals in recent years against Russia, we must remember Russia is "more Asian than European" as the author writes, and for that it is going to be "despised" by Western chauvinists. We must be aware of that endless fountain of racism and hypocrisy in the West whenever we hear the word "Russian" paired with something negative or supposedly scary in the media.

There is much to be hopeful about, as the book explains. The October Revolution's principles and ideals still "alive and well" in many countries for the simple reason they are "correct" and "reflect basic human dreams and aspirations". The reason the October Revolution remains uncontested as such an important event in modern history is because it was not fake like so many so-called uprisings and revolutions by plutocrats, power-mongers or the CIA. As Vltchek writes, "True Revolution is like an icebreaker.The revolutionaries are its crew". Such a uniquely Russian, uniquely Bolshevik view of revolution is a key part of what needs to be revived to overturn the stagnant global political order again."

- Harry J. Bentham

Andre Vltchek

EXPOSING LIES OF THE EMPIRE

Exposing Lies of The Empire is perhaps the most complete, and the most comprehensive account of the last several years, during which our planet has risen up and began its struggle against the Empire and its oppression. Vltchek takes us to all the continents, to slums and palaces, to the villages bombed into the ground, and to the front lines of the revolution. It alerts and provokes, clarifies and leads forward. It is a book of philosophy, a collection of exceptional investigative journalist reports,

and a manifesto. It will inspire millions. It will be quoted for centuries to come.

•••

"In an age of formula media, Andre Vltchek's work is truly exceptional -- fiercely independent and bracing in its challenges to the echoes and lies of the great power."

~ John Pilger

"Brave international correspondent and author Andre Vltchek has written countless essays and many books on the problems afflicting the world, from social injustice writ large, hidden institutionalized brutality, super- power hubris, and ecological murder, to the hypocrisy of entire cultures, beginning with the "Atlanticist civilization" that currently decimates the planet implementing the agendas of Washington's insatiable Neocons and a savage, cynical capitalism. Naturally, all of this is done in the name of those two sacred cows of all US world interventions: freedom and democracy...

This is one of Vltchek's most useful volumes, an anthology packed with the indispensable facts, first-hand knowledge, mature reflections, and righteous revolutionary furor necessary to combat the imperialist beast in all latitudes."

~ Patrice Greanville, *The Greanville Post*

"Exposing Lies of the Empire is a monumental work.

...the modus operandi of Andre Vltchek: go to the region, discover with purpose, and interview people from all walks of life to get the fullest possible local views, Weltanschauung, and insightful commentary on disparity along the power continuum.

... His reportages are about casting light on the ravages of western militarism and western rapacious capitalism for the rest of the world, pulling on the heart strings of the relatively comfortable people in the West...

In this book, readers can discover through Vltchek's words and photographs what life is like for the peoples embattled by insouciant capitalism in far-flung places: to name a few — Syria, Eritrea, China,

North Korea, Venezuela, Palestine, Viet Nam, and exotic locales few will have heard of, such as Kiribati.

Vltchek does not hold back as to what is harming people in the non-western lands. He points his finger — backed by evidence and compelling reasoning — at capitalists; capitalist's bloody henchmen, the military; empire's putschists and torturers; economic hitmen; collaborators; religious dogmatists; racists; the education (sic) system; media disinformation and propaganda; etc.

This is a book for everyone. Get it, read it, and become an informed citizen of earth. Find out what our broth- ers and sisters are resisting and solidarize with them. In particular, people who work within corporate journalism should read Exposing Lies of the Empire and find out what an authentic journalist really does."

~ Kim Petersen, *Dissident Voice*

AURORA

*"Aurora" is a short but emotionally charged
and 'outrageous' novel. It breaks many
taboos, especially those regarding Western,
particularly European culture, being refined
and superior to other cultures of the world.
Andre Vltchek does not think so, and he
shows how this – Western – culture can
indoctrinate, brainwash, and destroy.*

*The two main characters of "Aurora" are:
Hans G, the German-speaking head of a huge
European cultural institution, which is based*

in an unidentified Southeast Asian country (although many would guess that it is Indonesia), and his antagonist: a lady, a great local artist who literally escaped from her country to Venezuela and there married a revolutionary painter and a muralist. Her name is Aurora.

Hans G is not only the head of a cultural institute; he is also an intelligence officer, as well as a propagandist who uses 'art' and the funding of local artists for clear political motives: to depoliticize the country where he is based, to keep it obedient, ignorant, and passive.

Aurora sees clearly what Hans G. (and his 'culture') is doing to her country. She challenges him. She humiliates him publicly... For Aurora, the main reason for returning to her country is to find out the truth about her sister, who used to be another prominent progressive artist, but who was kidnapped, raped, tortured and murdered, mainly by those who were there to 'promote' that great European culture!

There are Mozart, Brecht and others appearing throughout the book. In the past, but also during these days, some of the greatest European musicians, writers and

painters were actually thoroughly destroyed and prostituted by the elites and by the Church. They were forced to produce technically brilliant but content-wise pathetic and toothless kitsch. Mozart and Brecht, sitting in a bar in an ancient Chilean city of Valparaiso, are discussing the past, the art, although they are mainly remembering that important encounter of Hans G with Aurora, which Mozart actually witnessed, as a ghost. In a way, both Mozart and Brecht are co-narrating "Aurora".
"Aurora" is easy to read, but structurally it is a multi-layered novel, short but conceptually complex. It is also full of dark humor.

●●●

"**Aurora** is a tremendous work. Aurora is what a literary work should be: fully human. It is also what used to be known as a major literary work because it's rare to its time. It represents a leading edge of consciousness, courage, and social need. A major work! ... I wish it could be 500 pages and dropped like a sonic boom on all the acclaimed literary centers of the world and be released like a climatic change for the good in the rest of the world."

~ Tony Christini, author of *Homefront*

"**Aurora** - Powerful! Poetic! Revolutionary – and downright telling truth to the core. Just wonderful! A masterpiece of its kind – Andre Vltchek has a style that makes the average man and woman shiver for its reality. He is a great philosopher, poet and story teller; a teller of stories of truth that leave behind a strong taste of conscience. Andre believes in the soul of trees – that makes him a very especially sensitive and sensible person. Chapeau!"

~ Peter Koenig, author of *Implosion* and co-author of *The World Order and Revolution*

"This is the finest novel that I have read over the last 25 years. It should be read in every secondary school in the world. This is a very model of what literature at its best could."

~ Sydney Shall

POINT OF NO RETURN

Point of No Return shows the world through the eyes of a war correspondence, visiting places that are rarely covered by the mainstream media, offering provocative points of view about the pitiful state of today's world, its disparities and scandalous post-colonial arrangement – including global market fundamentalism and neo-conservative culture that are overthrowing democratic principals that humanity has fought for over centuries.

"André Vltchek is a writer, the real thing, of the same caliber and breed as Hemingway and Malraux."

~ Catherine Merveilleux

"Andre Vltchek tells us about a world that few know, even when they think they do. That is because he tells the truth, vividly, with a keen sense of history, and with a perceptive eye that sees past surfaces to reality..."

~ Noam Chomsky

"Point of No Return is one of the great novels of the 21st century. It deserves a wide readership and serious critical appraisal. Over a half century ago, in his important book "American Moderns - From Rebellion to Conformity," the great literary critic Maxwell Geismar noted "Our best literary work has come from writers who are outside [the dominant] intellectual orbit, where [capitalist] panic has slowly subsided into inertia." Geismar anticipates Vltchek. Point of No Return explodes from that vital realm far beyond hegemonic control."

~ Tony Christini, author of *Homefront*

"Point of No Return is riveting."
~ Paulin Cesari, *Le Figaro*

"A fascinating look at the world through the eyes of a war correspondent – a world few of us know."
~ Eve Jackson, *France24*

"Once again, it's the context that makes the book. It is quite simply mind-boggling. Andre Vltchek knows very well what he's talking about (...). It is a book that cannot fail to move, a rich, strong and dense tale, by all means get a hold of a copy for an intelligent read!"
~ Yves Mabon

"Quite simply a masterpiece... All of the absurdity of our society, its lack of humanity and sense blows up in our face... All readers will feel touched by this narrative that speaks of liberty, choice and our place in the world."
~ Stephanie Morelli

"A splendid novel that will leave no one cold. The author skilfully takes us along on a mysterious and sorrowful journey. A gripping read. "

~ Patrick Martinez - *Radio Coteaux*

"André Vltchek offers an unsparing portrait of the world we live in. With his provocative outlook, he lays bare a situation that is really quite simple, and did not begin yesterday... Although this book does not raise easy questions, it is indeed easy to read, thanks to the wit and subtlety of its author. "

~ Françoise Bachelet

"Andre Vltchek's work has the incredible capacity of helping one break free from the culture of denial. His ability to translate reality into fiction is stunningly original and very personal. His work shocks you while at the same time reconnect you with the political realities of today. Wisdom can only from a clear understanding of the past and some brutal honesty. This is the purpose of Andre's political novels."

~ Anuradha Mittal, *The Oakland Institute*

CPSIA information can be obtained
at www.ICGtesting.com
Printed in the USA
LVHW08s1459210718
584527LV00001B/165/P